"*Surviving Teacher Burnout* is an invaluable res̶o̶u̶r̶c̶e̶ ̶f̶o̶ around weekly self-care activities make this book ̶e̶s̶p̶e̶c̶i̶a̶l̶l̶y̶ ̶p̶r̶a̶c̶t̶i̶c̶a̶l̶,̶ ̶a̶n̶d̶ ̶a̶n̶ ̶i̶n̶c̶r̶e̶d̶i̶b̶l̶e̶ accessible way to cultivate one's adult social and emotional learning (SEL) competencies while fostering well-being."

> —**Meena Srinivasan**, executive director of Transformative Educational Leadership (TEL); and author of *SEL Every Day, Teach Breathe Learn,* and *Integrating SEL into Every Classroom Quick Reference Guide*

"Amy Eva shares nuggets of wisdom gleaned from research on mindfulness, positive psychology, emotional intelligence, and flourishing—and translates them into manageable and engaging action steps for educators. *Surviving Teacher Burnout* offers an easy-to-use road map for busy teachers that unfolds gracefully over fifty-two weeks of practice. This book offers the gift of a year filled with opportunities for greater compassion, empathy, and self-care, and one that is sorely needed in this moment."

> —**Patricia Broderick, PhD**, assistant research professor at the Edna Bennett Pierce Prevention Research Center at Penn State University, professor emerita at West Chester University, and author of *Learning to BREATHE*

"*Surviving Teacher Burnout* is a hopeful, timely, and practical guide for teachers today who, in the face of unprecedented levels of job demands and stress, are seeking tools for self-care and for rekindling their passion for teaching. This easy-to-use, month-by-month guide is chock-full of wisdom and evidence-based practices that can support all who work in education not just to survive, but also to thrive."

> —**Robert W. Roeser, PhD**, Bennett Pierce professor of caring and compassion at Pennsylvania State University

"What a timely gift to the profession of teaching! This book turns the big idea of 'self-care' into practical, research-based strategies that educators can use to hit the reset button on their happiness in their careers. The weekly focus makes it so easy to use for busy professionals to not just survive, but to thrive in their careers. Highly recommend for not just teachers, but anyone working in schools!"

> —**Rebecca Branstetter, PhD**, school psychologist, and founder of The Thriving Students Collective

"*Surviving Teacher Burnout* is timely, relevant, and necessary. In these unprecedented times as teachers face the most difficult challenges in our history, Eva offers hope and proven strategies for building resilience by developing emotional mastery and applying it to improving our classroom interactions in ways that reduce stress and inspire learning. Highly recommended!"

> —**Patricia A. Jennings, PhD**, professor at the University of Virginia School of Education and Human Development; and author of several books, including *Mindfulness for Teachers*

"In the midst of one of the hardest times to be an educator, *Surviving Teacher Burnout* becomes an essential tool for educational professionals looking to reconnect with their purpose, build their resilience, and reclaim their well-being. Full of research-based and practical exercises, this book will become a daily companion for many teachers."

> —**Lorea Martínez, PhD**, award-winning founder and author of *Teaching with the HEART in Mind*, and faculty at Columbia University Teachers College

"Now is a time like no other for a book aimed at helping teachers weather these unprecedented times, and Eva's *Surviving Teacher Burnout* is a must-read for teachers who wish to have access to the information on evidence-based strategies for not only reducing their stress, but cultivating their own inner strength and resilience. Through its week-by-week, twelve-month guide, this book is a treasure trove of practical strategies that will not only reduce stress, but inspire teachers to be their best possible selves."

> —**Kimberly A. Schonert-Reichl, PhD**, NoVo Foundation Endowed Chair in Social and Emotional Learning, professor in the department of psychology at the University of Illinois at Chicago, and coeditor of *Handbook of Mindfulness in Education*

SURVIVING TEACHER BURNOUT

A Weekly Guide to Build Resilience,
Deal with Emotional Exhaustion &
Stay Inspired in the Classroom

AMY L. EVA, PHD

New Harbinger Publications, Inc.

Publisher's Note

NEW HARBINGER PUBLICATIONS is a registered trademark of New Harbinger Publications, Inc.

New Harbinger Publications is an employee-owned company.

Copyright © 2022 by Amy L. Eva
    New Harbinger Publications, Inc.
    5674 Shattuck Avenue
    Oakland, CA 94609
    www.newharbinger.com

Cover design by Sara Christian

Acquired by Wendy Millstine

Edited by Jennifer Eastman

Indexed by James Minkin

Library of Congress Cataloging-in-Publication Data on file

Printed in the United States of America

24 23 22

10 9 8 7 6 5 4 3 2 1   First Printing

Dedicated to all educational professionals working on behalf of students

Contents

Growing into Hope

Why did you pick up this book? You may feel world weary, exhausted. You may be asking yourself whether teaching is the job for you. Yet you want to feel hope. Despite your worst days, you may often feel committed to your work and your students, yet you crave some emotional sustenance for the days and weeks ahead. Your well-being may be critical, yet larger educational policies and practices leave you feeling helpless and deflated.

The fact is…teachers everywhere are experiencing burnout and demoralization—feeling dispirited, losing confidence and hope (Santoro 2018). The top words they're using to describe their feelings are *anxious, fearful, worried, overwhelmed,* and *sad* (Cipriano and Brackett 2020). While no one wants our pain to be contagious, this predicament can affect our students.

As a long-time educator, I've experienced all these emotions—often in cycles (across days, weeks, months, and years). Surrounded by students for much of my life, I've craved time and space to reconnect with myself, my purpose, and my pathway forward. Sometimes those moments of awareness arrived when I lay on my back in my dark cubby of an office. Other times I simply sat on the beach watching seagulls glide on pockets of wind. Regardless, I've learned that every time I decide to mentally *slow down* and live a more deliberate, conscious life—quietly present to both the beauty and suffering around me—I'm more grounded, peaceful, and dedicated to more hopeful, energizing exchanges with my students and colleagues.

Do you have moments of reckoning when you ask yourself, *What do I need to move forward with hope in this career?* You can decide to prioritize your well-being—it's not something that happens to you. You gather your courage and the tools you need, and you take another step. This daily commitment is a gift to yourself and your students. Your steadfast presence sustains them each day as you journey together, and they respond with energy, creativity, and growth that reinvigorates you. Teaching can be an upward emotional spiral again.

Research tells us that educators who practice mindfulness and other strategies for navigating challenging emotions report improvements in personal well-being and the ability to provide emotional support in their classrooms (Iancu et al. 2018). In fact, they're also more efficient in their use of instructional time—and their students tend to experience higher levels of motivation and engagement (Jennings et al. 2017). But knowing this isn't enough. Many educators struggle to commit to self-care practices—largely because institutional demands leave them with little time and energy to invest in themselves. There is a lot that we do not control as educators, yet we *can* draw on evidence-based strategies to navigate the day-to-day social-emotional dynamics of teaching.

I wrote this book because all the stops and starts I've experienced myself have shown me that my well-being is essential to being an inspired and *inspiring* teacher. I want to support you in sustaining greater emotional resilience in this vitally important, utterly exhausting, profoundly rewarding, humanizing work.

How to Use This Book

To keep it simple, this book guides you through twelve core themes spread over twelve months. Each week, you'll learn a new low-lift strategy and gain a tool for fostering well-being, resilience, and hope. The activity-based format is easy to navigate; you don't need to wade through the research or attend face-to-face programs or retreats. Using evidence-based principles drawn from psychology, sociology, and neuroscience, *Surviving Teacher Burnout* features one year of weekly actions, reflection questions, and resources to guide you now—and throughout your career.

During this year, it'll help to regularly check-in with yourself, asking *Where do I want to go? What's in my way right now?* And *What are my strengths, values, successes? How do they clarify my sense of purpose?* This book guides you to respond to such questions, giving you bite-sized insights each week to use immediately or whenever things get bumpy. I recommend using a journal alongside this book to track your actions, reflections, and growth.

This year, you'll build a new skill each month, exploring gratitude, optimism, mindfulness, forgiveness, empathic joy, self-compassion, purpose, curiosity, and other keys to well-being. Each week you'll read about a common challenge teachers face and an evidence-based insight or skill that provides a possible pathway around that obstacle. Then, there is one weekly "action"—supported and sustained by research. A few *guiding questions* prompt you to reflect on this action—with additional resources at your fingertips, as needed. In addition, there are a variety of tools (a list of the social and emotional learning competencies addressed by chapter, a group discussion guide, audio practices, etc.) on a webpage for this book. It can be found at http://www.newhar binger.com/49791. Last, a description of the *benefits* of each weekly action will encourage you to integrate them into your life over time. Together, these elements serve to bolster your confidence and provide a sense of empowerment as you negotiate the bumps, curves, and U-turns on your journey through this year.

Why this framework? This book is structured to catalyze hope. Researchers describe two fundamental components of hope: *agency thinking* and *pathway thinking*—a will and a way (Snyder 2002). When we're hopeful, we act with intention and confidence, keeping our goals in mind. That confidence helps us navigate obstacles, seeking alternative paths to meet those goals. With strategies and options, we can keep moving forward.

The book's format is simple, yet time pressure is real, so here's an important piece of advice. If you struggle to carve out space for yourself, you'd benefit from reading this book with a friend or one or more colleagues. Choose an accountability partner or group and check in each week—in person, by phone, or online. Schedule it. Keep the check-in brief. You might discuss the weekly reflection question, describe your response to the weekly action, and consider how you might share this practice with colleagues or students.

I invite you to begin this book with hope, which is more than just a feeling you have in fleeting moments. Hope is a commitment to believing in your ability to see your way forward—and a skill you can develop with time, care, and attention. As Joanna Macy says, "Active Hope is waking up to the beauty of life on whose behalf we can act."

MONTH 1

Understanding Your Emotions

Your emotions make you human. Even the unpleasant ones have a purpose. Don't lock them away. If you ignore them, they just get louder and angrier.

—Sabaa Tahir

Many of us have complicated relationships with our emotions based on our upbringing, cultural values, and wiring. For some, thinking and talking about emotions can feel psychologically threatening, risky, and even frightening. We may react impulsively without understanding what we feel, pretend the emotions aren't even there, or stuff them away. However, researchers tell us that regularly denying or suppressing emotions is generally not the best coping method (Compas et al. 2017).

Regardless of how we *feel* about our feelings, our emotions have a function. This month we will explore how we relate to our emotions—and what they can reveal to us.

1. We want students to understand the importance of identifying emotions + express them correctly. Understanding the difference in a feeling + an emotion.

Week 1: Identifying Your Emotions

Do you ever wake up with an emotional fog hanging over you? Whether you're teaching during challenging world events or facing a day-to-day struggle that's having a snowball effect on your emotions, no one likes to get out of bed dreading a school day.

Here's my immediate challenge: planning for a semester of online teaching. I feel a vague but powerful sense of overwhelm. (*Will I be ready? This is so much to learn, and I can barely keep up.*) When I consciously check in with myself and try to see my way through the haze, I can identify a web of feelings including:

- helplessness (*How will I reach them without being with them?*)

- frustration and anger (*I hate the stiltedness of online teaching; it's so inauthentic—especially now, when real human connection is desperately important.*)

- sadness and loneliness (*I'm so disconnected from people as it is.*)

- worry and fear (*Do I have the emotional groundedness and presence of mind to "see" my students and meet them where they are?*)

These are simply my most immediate feelings about online teaching—not to mention the state of the world. Of course, how I relate to these feelings is important, too.

A Pathway

One of our tasks in life is to learn how emotions play out in our minds and bodies so that we can better relate to ourselves and others. In simple terms, an emotion is a reaction to an event. And emotions can provide valuable information. If we pay attention to what we're feeling, we can use emotions as tools for guiding future decisions and actions (Keltner and Haidt 2001; Izard 2011).

"Emotional granularity," also called "emotion differentiation," is the ability to distinguish between specific emotions (Kashdan et al. 2015). It's a learnable skill that helps you cultivate resilience. When you can make fine-grained distinctions between emotions—particularly negative ones—you can learn to regulate your emotions, experience improved physical health, and become less likely to engage in destructive behaviors like drinking excessively when stressed or retaliating aggressively when someone hurts you (Barrett 2006; Smidt and Suvak 2015).

Ultimately, we can draw on our emotions to inform our behaviors. For example, consider my mélange of feelings about online teaching: my anger and frustration, for example, might lead me to action. In fact, it already has. I'm exploring new apps for fostering meaningful connection during online classes. My sense of overwhelm motivates me to carve out blocks of time for course prep in the mornings, and then to let go of the overwhelm for the rest of the day. My loneliness inspires me to reach out by phone or Facetime to at least one person each day, and I'm even writing an old-fashioned card to a dear friend from college this weekend.

And my fear about remaining present and emotionally grounded? Well, that's one of the reasons I'm writing this book in the first place. I want to feel a greater sense of peace and be more present to others, so I am sharing tools and insights with you on this journey.

It's also a meaningful way to connect and feel bonded with you and all the other educators out there in the world who struggle just like me.

An Action

To cultivate the resilience that comes with awareness of your emotions, briefly describe in your journal a few of the current challenges in your life. Then identify the emotions you feel about each challenge—anger, sadness, pride, worry, remorse, excitement, fear, and so on. List them all.

Next, rate each emotion's level of intensity to reflect the strength of your feelings (1–10, 1 = low intensity and 10 = very high intensity). Becoming aware of each emotion and how much it's affecting you can clarify how important this challenge may be to you. In addition, your ability to pinpoint your emotions may help you to move closer to an action or next step that aligns with your values.

Guiding Questions

To begin, choose one of the emotions you wrote down. Journal about this guiding question: How can the emotion inform your next steps for addressing this challenge? For example, ask yourself: *How might anger fuel action? Could sadness lead to empathy? Can worry inspire a plan?* Then select another emotion and follow the same process. Continue until you begin to see just how informative and helpful your emotions are.

Benefits

Over time, you may discover that your emotions can provide insights to navigating challenging circumstances. For example, if you witness someone being bullied and feel a general sense of "badness"—or even anger—that feeling might not call for a specific action on your part. But if you identify your response more specifically as something like "righteous indignation," it might lead you toward concrete action like reporting the incident and intervening to help the victim.

Emotions are information. As you become more aware of your emotions and learn to identify them with greater clarity and nuance, you can draw on them as data that influence your decisions and actions over time.

Additional Resources

- "Tame Reactive Emotions by Naming Them," *Mindful,* https://www.mindful.org /labels-help-tame-reactive-emotions-naming

- "Atlas of Emotions," http://atlasofemotions.org

Week 2: Being with Difficult Emotions

Years ago, when I began teaching teens about being mindful of emotions, I quickly learned that they totally misunderstood what "managing" their emotions meant. The point is not to battle the emotion for control, like one teen who envisioned himself strangling his personified "emotions" in a wrestling ring. Instead, it is more about holding that emotion gently in your hands, as you would a small bird or something precious and fragile.

Believing that emotions are bad and the (often) related strategy of trying to suppress threatening emotions have both been linked to mental health conditions like depression and anxiety (Ford and Gross 2019).

So how can we be with our emotions and express them without feeling like we're losing a battle for "control"? We can begin with awareness.

A Pathway

Learning to simply observe your emotions can prevent you from being caught up in the emotions in the first place. And along with awareness comes acceptance. You may not love the feelings you're experiencing, but you can be kind to yourself while you're feeling them. Ignoring or suppressing guilt, sadness, or shame can cause further suffering, but acknowledging those emotions can ease a little of the pressure you feel.

One of the most practical ways to observe and accept your emotions is through writing. Your writing space becomes a container for your emotions—it gives you a certain psychological distance from them as well as a way to gently hold them near you. Expressive writing is simple—write for ten to twenty minutes straight with no concern for grammar or spelling and explore the emotions you experience as you describe a stressful event.

If you're someone who journals, you may already find yourself drawn to writing as a tool for identifying strong emotions. Naming an emotion may create some distance from it; it loses some of its intensity. Research suggests that labeling an emotion may reduce activation of your amygdala, the emotion center of the brain, and increase activation in part of your prefrontal cortex—a region associated with planning and impulse control (Lieberman et al. 2007). Specifically, when researchers measured adults' brain activity as they labeled their emotions while writing, they found that effects to the prefrontal cortex and amygdala were associated with improvements in physical symptoms, depression, and life satisfaction three months later (Memarian et al. 2017).

You may not be surprised to learn that our students also tend to respond similarly—whether they're suppressing or expressing emotions. A review of 212 studies, featuring 80,000 children and adolescents, tells us that disengagement, suppression, and denial are all linked to poorer psychological health (Compas et al. 2017). Meanwhile, students who engage in guided expressive writing activities—creating narratives about challenging events, reflecting on their emotions, and advising others on how to navigate difficult emotions—generally experience greater mental health (Torre and Lieberman 2018).

An Action

This week, when you experience a stressful event, try not to push away your feelings. Write about the event several times this week for ten to twenty minutes; you may find yourself adding, revising, and formulating the event in your mind as you explore your thoughts and feelings. Alternatively, write about several different events—whatever works for you.

Guiding Questions

Pull out your journal again and describe your experience with expressive writing. What did you observe? After you identify what you were feeling and why, do you notice a shift in the intensity of your feelings?

Benefits

In one study of teachers writing about emotionally charged experiences with their students, researchers found that repeatedly writing narratives about the incident decreased teachers' feelings of helplessness and lessened the intensity of their negative emotions about the students and situations. These same teachers also reported later feeling more confident and competent with classroom management (Tal et al. 2019).

Decades of research tells us that people who write about difficult events experience benefits to both their physical health—like fewer doctor visits and a healthier immune system—and their mental health, including lowered depression and anxiety and increased life satisfaction (Pennebaker 2018). We can all benefit from "permission to feel" and safe spaces to express our emotions. As we learn to identify and describe our feelings, they lose some of their power—and that can lead us to make the next best decision each day.

Additional Resources

- Marc Brackett, *Permission to Feel: Unlocking the Power of Emotions to Help Our Kids, Ourselves, and Our Society Thrive*

- "Research Matters: A 'Write' Way to Address Trauma," *Educational Leadership,* https://www.ascd.org/el/articles/research-matters-a-write-way-to-address-trauma

Week 3: Working with Anger

Many of those in the teaching force are women. How comfortable are they with their anger? Regardless of our gender, we teachers are supposed to be "good" people, right? We're in this line of work because we *care*. So what do we do with our frustration, annoyance, or—dare I say it—our rage?

It's helpful to look at why most humans get angry in the first place. We experience anger (Farouk 2010) when:

- we sense a threat to self (*This student makes me feel unsafe.*)

- we perceive a potentially blocked goal (*All this paperwork keeps me from doing the real work of teaching.*)

- we feel someone or something deserves blame (*This "professional development" is a total waste of my time. The district is so out of touch with my needs.*)

- we believe something is unfair or unjust (*Without these resources, over half of my students are set up for failure.*)

After researcher Shaalan Farouk (2010) asked fifty-two elementary teachers to track their "anger events" over a two-week period, they identified two primary types of teacher anger. First, teachers talked about their in-the-moment expression of "restricted" anger. This form of anger was geared more toward students when teachers perceived a goal being blocked, and they felt frustration or levelled blame, such as when a student was unresponsive to their efforts.

On the other hand, when teachers experienced anger toward adults, like parents or colleagues, they tended to experience "elaborated anger," which they did not immediately express—instead, it bubbled away in their heads over time. Elaborated anger often coincided with blame, a sense of feeling threatened, or a perception of unjust outcomes.

How can we navigate and work with that anger?

A Pathway

Bottom line: researchers associate lower teacher self-efficacy with anger (Burić et al. 2020). When we sense threats to our identity as a teacher and our capacity to do good work, we're more likely to get mad. Anger tends to proceed down different pathways depending on the way we view ourselves in relation to the people around us—students, other teachers, parents, administrators, policy makers (Meloy-Miller et al. 2018). "Hostile" anger results when we have an unhealthy view of ourselves—either inflated or collapsed. We either "inflate" and respond aggressively (*I'll find a way to get back at them.*) or "collapse" and internalize our anger (*Maybe I deserved to be treated this way.*).

On the other hand, we tend to express more "benevolent" anger when we have a more balanced view of ourselves in relationship to others (Meloy-Miller et al. 2018). For example, if I see that my student isn't threatening me with their raised voice and defiant tone, but that they feel disempowered in some way, I can respond with greater understanding and support them with a plan to move forward with their late essay or their struggle with attendance. This approach can lead to conflict resolution, problem solving, or even advocacy on behalf of your students (Meloy-Miller et al. 2018).

Now, consider how we can shift our view of ourselves in relationship to those who pique our anger so that hostile anger can dissipate and be replaced with productive and benevolent anger. There are several ways to address anger—examining triggers, observing our body's response when we're angry, distracting ourselves, taking a time-out, exercising, mindfully observing our own anger, and engaging in body-relaxation techniques. These can all be useful strategies, but the most well-researched method for navigating anger draws on cognitive behavioral therapy (CBT) (Lee and DiGiuseppe 2017). This involves noting your thought patterns and belief patterns over time and considering how they influence your emotions and behaviors. According to CBT, we can engage in irrational thought patterns called "cognitive distortions":

- Should Statements: *This shouldn't have happened, and…*

- Catastrophizing (Magnification): *It's awful that it did, and I can't stand it, and…*

- Personalizing: *It's all my fault!*

- Fortune-telling: *This will never get better!*

My go-to cognitive distortion is *personalizing,* which is a way of internalizing my anger. It's my fault that my student is upset; if I just would have shifted my tone, we wouldn't have had this conflict. I'm also skilled at catastrophizing with a dose of fortune-telling: *How could the district have added even more unnecessary paperwork to my pile?! I'm totally overwhelmed, and I'll never get this done.*

An Action

Do you typically default to one of the common cognitive distortions? If you're unsure of your irrational belief patterns, use this week to simply track and write down some of the things you say to yourself each day—particularly in stressful times.

Guiding Questions

After you have tracked your angry thoughts this week, consider how these statements reflect your view of yourself as you relate to students, colleagues, administrators, and parents. Is there a way to reframe these statements so you feel a stronger sense of yourself and your ability to do your job? For example, *I wish this conflict hadn't happened, but it did. How can I move forward with this student?* Or *Maybe it's not all my fault; rather than blaming myself or someone else, I can look at the facts and see how we both contributed to this misunderstanding.*

Benefits

With practice, we can recognize our faulty thinking patterns and redirect them. With a more balanced perspective, it's possible to channel anger, an emotion that can direct us to act, so that we can use our anger for the good. In fact, researchers point to the many benefits of anger expression—including creativity, enhanced job performance, and even increased optimism (Kashdan and Biswas-Diener 2014). As poet Audre Lorde once said, "Anger is loaded with information and energy.... Focused with precision it can become a powerful source of energy serving progress and change."

Additional Resources

- "Eleven Anger Management Strategies to Help You Calm Down," *verywellmind,* https://www.verywellmind.com/anger-management-strategies-4178870

- "What Are Cognitive Distortions?," *Positive Psychology,* https://positive psychology.com/cognitive-distortions

---

Week 4: Savoring Positive Emotions

One of my teacher-friends recently chronicled her massive list of daily responsibilities: teach and plan lessons, grade, answer student and parent emails, write reports, attend meetings, teach advisory…plus twenty more items. She ended her long post with a pointed question aimed at her school district's administrators: "Why do you keep reminding me to care for myself and my family during these difficult times?" It hit me like a brick.

With the ongoing sense of urgency many teachers feel, self-care doesn't always seem realistic—particularly when it feels like another directive from leadership. Researchers claim that "time pressure" may be one of the strongest predictors of teachers' emotional exhaustion and burnout (Jennings et al. 2013). So how do you slow down and find joy amid a relentless pull to perform?

A Pathway

When teachers experience positive emotions like joy, contentment, or enthusiasm, they experience less stress and burnout as well as a stronger sense of self-efficacy and emotional resilience (Frenzel et al. 2009; Skaalvik and Skaalvik 2010). And positive psychology researcher Sonja Lyubomirsky claims that close to half of our happiness (40 percent) depends on our daily activities (see Additional Resources).

Here's the good news: there are simple ways to trick your brain into getting more time and meaning out of each day's events. Multiple studies tell us that taking time to notice and appreciate positive experiences leads to greater happiness. "Savoring" is a way to slow down and take in positive emotions and experiences. Although we talk a lot about how to manage unpleasant emotions, research tells us that savoring turns that idea on its head. It is an emotion regulation strategy that focuses on the positive and can result in an emotion uplift. When you ramp up your experiences of savoring, you are more likely to report an increase in positive life events, or uplifts, for as long as three months afterward (Tugade and Fredrickson 2007).

Based on extensive research, Fred B. Bryant and Joseph Veroff identified a range of savoring activities that can increase your enjoyment of the positive events in your life (see Additional Resources). Here are a just a few:

- Sharing with others: inviting others to share positive experiences and expressing how much you value moments together (e.g., acknowledging the joy you feel when you go for a walk or a run with friends or colleagues).

- Memory building: consciously capturing and storing positive memories so that you can reminisce about a special experience (e.g., I still have a vivid memory of the white lights, artwork, and dark walls of my high school students' "Poetry Café" where we celebrated their creative voices).

- Sensory sharpening: focusing on your senses while blocking out other stimuli from your environment (e.g., relishing in the scent of freshly ground coffee, feeling the heat of the cup in your hands, experiencing the rich flavor and warmth of the liquid as it moves down your throat).

- Self-congratulation: taking pride in your accomplishments while reflecting on the outcomes of your efforts and the positive impact you have on others (e.g., doing a victory dance when all your students pass that math test or basking in the glory of having graded all those papers so thoughtfully).

- Behavioral expression: reinforcing the beauty of the moment by laughing, jumping up and down, or verbalizing your appreciation (e.g., I like to scamper around the house with my goofy cats, making silly vocalizations).

- Absorption: relaxing, slowing down, and letting go of thoughts—being in the present moment (e.g., instead of checking your email between classes, lingering a moment over the taste of something sweet or walking outside and taking three long, deep breaths).

When we savor, we aren't only feeling pleasure but also acknowledging that pleasure and extending our enjoyment of that moment. According to psychologist Fred Bryant, savoring can become "an acquired skill" with time and practice.

An Action

Savor things that bring you joy this week. Spend several minutes savoring two pleasant experiences a day to make them last for as long as possible. For example, take time to enjoy your cup of tea, a warm conversation with a friend, a hug, the sound of the rain—whatever you choose.

Guiding Questions

What activities or events did you savor? What was it like to be focused and present to a moment of joy or contentment? Describe your experiences in your journal, savoring them even more by writing about them.

Benefits

As you continue to experiment with your repertoire of savoring strategies, share them with your students. Although there isn't a lot of research on students' go-to savoring strategies, we are learning that teens seem to be particularly drawn to both "sharing with others" and "self-congratulation" (Chadwick et al. 2020). And researchers clearly link teacher enjoyment with student enjoyment in the classroom (Frenzel et al. 2009). Savoring gives you a wonderful opportunity to extend moments of joy inside and outside the classroom. Your enjoyment and enthusiasm will be contagious.

Additional Resources

- Fred B. Bryant and Joseph Veroff, *Savoring: A New Model of Positive Experience*

- Sonja Lyubomirsky, *The How of Happiness: A New Approach to Getting the Life You Want*

Being with Life—As It Is

Every time you know you're lost, you're found.

—Adyashanti

During my years as a teacher educator, I opened each class with a few moments of mindfulness. Initially, many of my students expressed concern about their ability to sit with their thoughts: "Amy, I can't do it; my mind wanders too much. I can't stop thinking." Well, that's exactly the point! It's not about controlling your thoughts. All you are doing is observing them, witnessing them, noticing them.

The truth is our minds wander about 47 percent of the time. After studying over five thousand adults in eighty-three different countries, Matthew Killingsworth and Daniel Gilbert (2010) tell us that "a human mind is a wandering mind." And a wandering mind tends to be an "unhappy mind." Just a few minutes of silence can yield questions, criticisms, doubts, and insecurities. We recall what went wrong and make plans to make things "right." We speculate about possible outcomes and remind ourselves how we continually fall short of our expectations.

Yet research suggests that mindfulness, the practice of nonjudgmental present-moment awareness, can support teachers' mental health and emotion regulation while enhancing their awareness, focus, working memory, physical health, and belief in themselves (Emerson et al. 2017; Jennings et al. 2013; Lomas et al. 2017; Roeser et al. 2013; Schussler et al. 2016). So, this month we are going to focus on being with our experiences—just as they are.

Week 5: Checking In with Yourself

Do you sometimes feel like you've lost yourself in the flow of a teaching day? Many teachers find all their energy dispersing outward, so it can be challenging to collect themselves during the daily frenzy. (*Where am I? Am I still here?*) When this happens, it can be reassuring to pause and reconnect with your body. (*Ah, here I am. Feet on the ground, head up, shoulders back, gathering my breath.*)

Teaching requires many different skills practiced all at once—not to mention those super-human "eyes at the back of our heads." Anyone who has taught for more than a few hours knows that it also requires on-your-toes flexibility, in the moment, every day. There are always competing priorities, voices, and demands.

During my first year of teaching, I sometimes stole away from the hubbub during my lunch break, closed my office door for five minutes, turned off the lights, and lay on my back—calming my overstimulated body. I was caught up in the needs, lives, and stories of my 163 ninth and tenth graders, and I knew the best thing I could do for myself was to stop and just "be" for a moment, before reengaging with those kids I loved.

Even now it can take me a few hours to "come down" from an exhausting/exhilarating few hours of teaching. Thinking back to those early years, I realize I was also intuitively searching for grounding. I tend to live in my head, so lying on the ground helped me reconnect with my body and reboot my nervous system. Teaching can also be physical work; we're constantly moving, adjusting, approaching, and retreating as we read the needs of students. So how do you check in and reconnect with your body?

A Pathway

During those five-minute body breaks on my office floor, I was unwittingly finding my way to a mindfulness practice. Mindfulness is present-moment awareness that is kind, curious, and nonjudgmental. At that time, I was homing in on the present-moment-awareness aspect of mindfulness, simply being with my body. The kind, curious component would come later—and is still a challenge. (*Well, here I am, and this is what I'm feeling right now—my shoulder aches, my body feels weak, and I'm going to lie here quietly and feel my breath.*)

One of the key benefits of "being with" and observing your body responses is that it provides an opportunity to detach from your head a little bit. Mindfulness practices give us permission to stop and pause. If we are continuously *doing*—running round and round in our little hamster wheels—we can lose connection with who we are as human beings.

If you can't close a door and turn off the lights in the middle of a school day, here is one thing to do. In her book *Mindfulness for Teachers,* researcher Patricia Jennings (see Additional Resources) describes a way to check in with yourself during the flow of a day—whether you are preparing to begin a class, monitoring small-group discussions, or transitioning between activities. She calls it "centering." Stand, find the center of gravity in your abdomen (two inches below your navel and about an inch into your body), and focus on this point while feeling your feet solidly on the ground. You can also use it—in the moment—when you want to feel more emotionally grounded and prepared to respond (rather than react) to a challenge.

However, if you would like to incorporate a brief yet thorough check-in with your body, take a time-out at lunch, during a free period, or at the start or end of the day. Slow down and mentally tend to your whole body—acknowledging any tension you feel while shifting away from the commotion in your head.

An Action

This week, practice engaging in a brief "body scan" each day. In a body scan, you typically lie on your back and deliberately move your attention through your body—concentrating on every body part in turn, relaxing them one at a time. For example, focus on your head and relax the muscles of your face, then move your focus to your neck, then shoulders, and so on, one body part at a time, all the way to your toes. You can find an audio clip of a body scan meditation at http://www.newharbinger.com/49791. You might also consider a longer body scan before you sleep at night.

Guiding Questions

As you practice checking in with your body this week, where do you notice tension? Journal about how it feels to mentally connect with the parts of your body that feel tense or relaxed. How do you feel after completing a short body scan? Do you sense any changes in body sensations, thoughts, or feelings?

Benefits

Of all mindfulness practices, the body scan is one of the most popular—and it's a great introduction to mindfulness. A body scan shifts us away from our thoughts to focus on physical sensations.

Interoception is the ability to accurately detect sensations that arise in our bodies. With time, we can sharpen this sensory skill. In fact, in one study, adults who practiced body scans for twenty minutes every day for eight weeks improved their interoception. They could feel their heartbeat more clearly and identify other sensations more accurately (Fischer et al. 2017). Being able to do this is key to psychological well-being. When we can see ourselves more clearly—and, in this case, feel our own presence more accurately through our senses—we experience more agency in our own lives (Farb et al. 2015).

When you regularly engage in body scans, you may experience less stress and anxiety, and even significantly reduce symptoms of depression (Corbett et al. 2019). Body scan practices (along with calm breathing, focused attention, and relaxation) can be particularly helpful to teachers as they navigate challenging student behaviors in the classroom (Haydon et al. 2019). Ultimately, as teachers consciously practice observing their moment-to-moment experiences with curiosity, openness, and kindness, they can learn to navigate stress with more detachment and less anxiety (Lomas et al. 2017).

Additional Resources

- Patricia Jennings, *Mindfulness for Teachers: Simple Skills for Peace and Productivity in the Classroom*

- "A Three-Minute Body Scan to Cultivate Mindfulness," *Mindful Magazine,* https://www.mindful.org/a-3-minute-body-scan-meditation-to-cultivate-mindfulness

- "Body Scan for Sleep," *Greater Good in Education,* https://ggie.berkeley.edu/practice/body-scan-for-sleep

---

Week 6: Observing Your Emotions

I've always been a highly sensitive person. I tend to carry the burdens of the world in my heart and body. Can you relate? Do you feel emotions deeply? If so, how do you navigate them?

Emotion researcher James Gross defines *emotion regulation* as "the processes by which individuals influence which emotions they have, when they have them, and how they experience and express these emotions" (1998, 275). If we struggle to regulate our emotions and mask them with a happy (or at least neutral) face, we may find ourselves engaging in *emotional labor*—"the management of feeling to create a publicly observable facial and bodily display" (Hochschild 1983, 7).

Teachers' ability to regulate their emotions can be linked to their job satisfaction (Brackett et al. 2010). Further, emotional labor requires effort that may lead to burnout—as well as stress, exhaustion, problems with physical health, and a sense of inauthenticity (Hochschild 1983; Taxer and Frenzel 2015). Research also suggests that when teachers suppress their emotions or fake emotions they aren't feeling (also called "surface acting"), they may end up experiencing more negative emotions like anxiety, anger, and frustration (M. Lee et al. 2016).

So where is the happy balance? How do we learn to be with our emotions without becoming swept up in them? How do we avoid the exhaustion associated with "faking it" in front of students and colleagues so that we don't end up collapsing on the couch by dinnertime?

A Pathway

Last week you practiced bringing your awareness to your body and sensory experience. Now we are focusing on our vast and complex internal world—the emotional terrain you traverse each day. When we aren't aware of our inner world, that world can dictate how we interact with and respond to others—without us having a lot of choice in the matter. When we experience challenging emotions, we may not even be fully conscious of them. However, when we begin to actively observe our emotions, we are able to navigate that stress a bit better. Opening ourselves to our emotional experiences may feel risky, but it's tempered when we practice *equanimity.*

One of the key skills we learn as we practice mindful awareness is equanimity: the ability to allow sensory and emotional experiences to come and go without suppressing or avoiding them (Young 2016). We also learn not to overidentify with an experience or make it too personal. Here's how equanimity is expressed: *Okay, I'm angry right now; I feel it in my body here and here, and I'm going to watch it move through me; I'm not going to be swept up in it.*

As we learn to quietly witness our feelings as they play out in our bodies—watching them from the sidelines—something happens in our heads; brain activation patterns shift. The amygdala is aroused when you detect and react to emotions, especially difficult or strong emotions like fear, but following mindfulness training, this part of the brain is typically less activated and has less gray matter density. In addition, after mindfulness training, the prefrontal cortex (associated with planning, emotion regulation, and decision making) becomes more activated (Goldin and Gross 2010; Hölzel et al. 2011).

Apart from notable brain changes, mindfulness practice appears to enhance our ability to navigate and regulate emotions. Adults who practice mindfulness seem to be more flexible and adaptive—taking emotions as they come; they tend to recover from difficult emotions more quickly and feel less intense distress (Roemer et al. 2015).

An Action

Here is a brief set of steps for observing your feelings this week. The acronym RAIN (originally created twenty years ago by Michele McDonald) will help you to remember a simple framework for observing our emotions that psychologist and teacher Tara Brach has adapted and shared widely (see Additional Resources):

1. Recognize what is going on. (*My chest is tightening, and heat is moving through my body.*)

2. Allow the experience to be there, just as it is. (*I am upset—embarrassed, frustrated, even ashamed—and that's okay.*)

3. Investigate with kindness, interest, and care. (*Where do I feel this most? Why? Is this response like others I have had in this situation? How can I take care of myself right now?*)

4. Natural awareness, which comes from not identifying with the experience. (*I feel this in my body, and it will pass. I don't need to be swept away by this feeling—it is what it is.*)

Practice these four steps, in order, at least once a day. Pause, notice the feelings you are experiencing in your body. Accept them as they are. Kindly ask yourself about the experience: *What is happening?* And, finally, practice equanimity—be *with* the experience without being caught up *in* it.

Guiding Questions

How do you feel while you are running through these steps? Do you notice a shift in the intensity of your feelings? Journal about which of the four steps is most challenging for you, and why.

Benefits

As you begin to step back and watch what's happening in your emotional body, you may find yourself able to detach from your feelings a bit. The more I practice mindful awareness, the more I am able to ride my emotions like waves—rather than finding myself toppled over by them.

Reviews of multiple mindfulness studies with educators suggest that mindfulness practice may have a positive effect on teachers' mental health, emotion regulation, job performance, and physical health—including their sleep quality (Frank et al. 2015; Klingbeil and Renshaw 2018; Lomas et al. 2017). Mindfulness practice can also be effective at reducing teachers' sense of "time pressure" and stress (Jennings et al. 2013). And a review of research suggests that emotion regulation—including emotional awareness, recognition, and understanding—may be the key to ultimately reducing stress and enhancing teachers' social and emotional competence in the classroom (Emerson et al. 2017).

What does the "mindful self" look like in school relationships? The bonus here is that mindful awareness seems to also enhance our ability to connect with our students. When we are less caught up in our own emotional struggles, we are more likely to reach out with greater empathy and compassion (Lavy and Berkovich-Ohana 2020). So, when we practice mindfulness, we're opening our potential to be with others in ways that are more kind, calm, and caring (Klingbeil and Renshaw 2018).

Additional Resources

- Tara Brach, *Radical Compassion: Learning to Love Yourself and Your World with the Practice of RAIN*

- "Practice the RAIN Meditation with Tara Brach," *Mindful Magazine,* https://www .mindful.org/investigate-anxiety-with-tara-brachs-rain-practice

---

Week 7: Noticing Your Thoughts

Over fifteen years ago, I started "studying" mindfulness because I also have an honorary PhD in worry. I've struggled in my life with anxiety and overthinking. My busy, monkey brain goes at it regularly—moving through next week's meetings; upping the ante by reviewing the entire month's deadlines; and then spinning backward, forward, and back again as I ruminate about a challenging relationship with a colleague.

Those of us who struggle with worry and rumination tend to also struggle with sleep, which can ultimately affect our health and well-being (Clancy et al. 2020). Of course, as our workloads increase at school, researchers are finding that we're challenged to psychologically detach. "Work-related rumination" finds its way through the delicate boundaries between work and home life, seeping into our personal lives (Türktorun et al. 2020).

Fortunately, I have learned to fall into my mindfulness practice when this happens late at night, and it has become a soothing balm to my restless and weary mind. Mindful awareness can reduce worry and rumination—patterns of thinking linked to depression (Parmentier et al. 2019).

A Pathway

In fact, an extensive review of research indicates that "awareness"—attentiveness to our environment and our thoughts, feelings, and emotions—is one of the core dimensions of psychological well-being, and it's something that we can develop through mental training (Dahl et al. 2020). When we suddenly catch ourselves on autopilot—with busy minds in a whirl of activity—we're experiencing what researchers call "meta-awareness." Simply recognizing these thoughts or feelings can remove you, to some degree, from the internal fray.

It's one thing to experience a distracted or wandering mind, but it's another to ruminate—to have seemingly uncontrollable, repetitive, and intrusive thoughts (Parmentier et al. 2019). Like that irritating song you can't get out of your head, a thought (or series of thoughts) about a negative experience plagues us, unrelenting: *Why did I do that? How did it affect my colleagues? Will they ever view me in the same way?*

"Maladaptive" rumination can feature big-picture and high-level reflections about who you are and how you feel, which can lead to negative generalizations (*I'm a bad teacher; I hate my job*). However, researchers link mindful awareness to "adaptive" rumination—more specific and concrete thoughts about a negative event, with a greater focus on the practical "how" and the details behind the action. In other words, you may see that challenging exchange with a colleague more objectively—rather than spinning on its deeper significance and possible repercussions (Heeren and Philippot 2011).

When I learned that mindful awareness could shift the way we think, it didn't surprise me at all. When we practice mindful awareness, we regularly return to focusing on the tangible "here and now," the present. More importantly, we practice curiosity—rather than judgment of our thoughts.

And more good news! In one study, researchers found that teachers participating in randomized controlled trials featuring mindfulness training experienced less rumination about work when teachers were at home (Crain et al. 2017). As a result, educators reported more sleep on weekdays, better sleep quality, less insomnia, and better moods overall.

An Action

With this in mind, let's try two different mindfulness practices this week. Each practice draws on a different attentional skill set—"open awareness" or "focused attention" (Zajoncs 2016).

First, try "open awareness." In this case, all you need to do is spend a few minutes a day gently labeling and letting go of your thoughts as they pass through your mind. Watch them come and go (like clouds passing overhead). As you observe your thoughts, you might say "thinking," "wondering," "planning," or "remembering"—whatever works for you. This doesn't mean that you won't inevitably pause and fixate on a thought—*When am I going to finish all this grading?* or *Why am I so sleepy today?*—but the idea is to let that thought pass and to open yourself to other thoughts as they come and go.

Second, if you find that you would prefer not to label and observe your thoughts, you can shift your goal, drawing instead on the cognitive mechanism of "focused attention." Here, you anchor your attention on a specific target apart from your thoughts. For example, you might focus on what it feels like to take ten breaths, in and out. Or you might direct your attention outside of your body to a sound—a bird singing outdoors or traffic passing. Again, this doesn't mean that you won't notice yourself thinking midway through the first or second breath or seconds after you hear that bird singing. Your key purpose is to practice gently and nonjudgmentally redirecting your attention—over and over—to your breath or to a sound. This quiet, caring practice of redirecting your attention is at the heart of mindfulness.

Guiding Questions

What were the benefits and challenges you experienced when practicing open awareness of your thoughts versus focused attention on your breath or on a sound? Did you find yourself gravitating to one practice more than the other? Why? Use these questions to reflect on your experiences in your journal.

Benefits

I find that observing my thoughts can be just enough to shift me away from an oncoming mental tailspin of sorts. However, when I'm in the thick of it and ruminating late at night, I often rely on focused attention practices—finding a different way to anchor my focus on breath, body sensations, or sounds. Over time, mindfulness practice can give us the capacity to step outside of our internal experiences with greater detachment. Although this is very "internal" work or "mental training," it can set the stage for a more flexible, nimble, and adaptive approach to life and relationships in general.

In fact, a massive review of research now tells us that there is one quality or way of being that is most predictive of happy and successful relationships (particularly those with our family and our romantic partners). Did I pique your interest?

A review of 174 studies featuring over 44,000 adults suggests that the key to successful relationships is actually "psychological flexibility" (Daks and Rogge 2020). What does this look like? Being more open and accepting, aware of the present moment, less likely to ruminate (surprise, surprise!), and able to step back from a challenge to view it in context. Sound familiar?

The evidence is in. We can improve our psychological flexibility, and mindfulness is one way to do it.

Additional Resources

- "A Meditation on Observing Thoughts, Nonjudgmentally," *Mindful Magazine,* https://www.mindful.org/a-meditation-on-observing-thoughts-non-judgmentally

- "Mindful Breathing for Adults," *Greater Good in Education,* https://ggie.berkeley .edu/practice/mindful-breathing-for-adults

Week 8: Becoming More Mindful of Others

Many of your colleagues may roll their eyes when they hear the word "mindfulness." Has mindfulness become a watered-down pop culture trend? A stress-management tool? A method for controlling student behavior? Van Gordon and Shonin (2020) claim that mindfulness, in its current Westernized formulation, might be best described as nothing more than "attention-based training."

Even worse, practitioners who critique secularized mindfulness claim that it can become a dangerously self-indulgent practice (Baer 2015). They have a point. I'm picturing a central character from the television show *Billions* sitting alone on their yoga mat in the early morning—calmly meditating—before they launch into another day of cold corporate takedowns. If we consider mindfulness purely as an internal tool, a means to an end, we lose a sense of how it can connect us to each other.

A Pathway

Despite my (very Western) training as a researcher who tracks the benefits and outcomes of mindfulness "interventions," I see and experience mindfulness as both a daily practice and a disposition—a way of engaging life and those around me. Researchers Siyin Chen and Christian H. Jordan (2020) recently studied the effects of two approaches to mindfulness training—one focused more on human ethics and one more technical and secularized. They led similar mindfulness practices across both groups, focusing on breath, body sensations, and emotions. However, they added language about human connection and interdependence in the ethical group, emphasizing the importance of doing no harm and extending kindness and gratitude to others. Chen and Jordan found that adults who received the ethical instructions expressed a greater willingness to donate to a charity (2020).

Mindfulness isn't just about individual practice or experience; it encompasses a rich tradition of community and communion. Research indicates that simple awareness practices can even help disrupt some of our more biased ways of thinking (Lueke and Gibson 2014; Parks et al. 2017). When we are more attuned and aware, we can consciously choose how we engage with one another. Mindfulness practice can make us more aware of the quick assumptions we make based on gender, age, and race in a given moment—helping us to slow down and become more curious and open to understanding others.

In another groundbreaking study, Tania Singer and her colleagues examined the effects of different forms of mindfulness practice (i.e., both individual, attention-based practices and pair- or group-based practices drawing on active listening skills) on participants' reported stress and well-being. Her team discovered that interactive practices (targeting compassion and perspective-taking) yielded greater individual health benefits (including reduced stress) and enhanced participants' compassion and sense of social connectedness (Singer and Engert 2018).

Two large reviews of mindfulness studies, featuring a range of practices at different intensity levels, positively linked mindfulness to prosocial behavior like kindness and altruism (Donald et al. 2019) and prosocial emotions like empathy and compassion (Luberto et al. 2018). Why would mindfulness lead to kindness? We are learning that teachers describe a different relationship with time after mindfulness training. When we slow down and pause during the flow of our workday, we can shift the social-emotional dynamics in our classroom and encourage a more positive, prosocial climate (Mackenzie et al. 2020).

An Action

This week, take a few minutes to become more aware of your connection to others. Recall one or two students or colleagues you know. Picture their faces. What experiences do you share with this person or people? Do you have similar hopes? Feelings? Imagine them experiencing joy. Consider some of their strengths and interests. With curiosity and nonjudgment, consider how you might get to know them better. An audio clip of a mindfulness script can be found at http://www.newharbinger.com/49791.

Guiding Questions

After spending a few minutes picturing your students or colleagues, journal for a few minutes by responding to the following: What role do they play in your classroom or school? How do they relate to others? What are you learning from them? Do you notice any changes in yourself as you relate to them now? Throughout the coming week?

And at this point in the month, ask yourself how you view mindfulness in general. Do you see mindfulness as a "path"—a way of being with yourself and the world, a pursuit of wisdom? Or do you see it (at least right now) more as a "tool"—a useful tool with the potential to enrich your life the more you use it?

If you agree that it is a way of "being with life—as it is," how might you integrate mindfulness into your days so that you are more present—not only to yourself, but also to the human beings around you?

Benefits

Mindfulness practice can shift the way we view our students and improve the way we teach. Researchers are learning that mindfulness benefits teachers' sense of well-being as well as their social-emotional competence, which can lead to more supportive teacher-student relationships and more positive learning experiences at school (Jennings and Greenberg 2009).

New teachers who participated in about two months of mindfulness practice demonstrated stronger instructional supports and greater classroom organization when compared to their counterparts (Hirshberg et al. 2020). After engaging in several weeks of mindfulness practice, another group of teachers reported that they were more likely to view challenging students positively—and more likely to forgive them (C. Taylor et al. 2016).

Of course, when describing the research-based benefits of mindfulness, we inevitably stumble into a more instrumentalist view. In other words, *What will this thing do for me—and my students?* Yes, we can call it a "tool," but it's so important to remember that it can ultimately enhance our day-to-day awareness and interactions as it becomes a disposition or a way of being.

I believe strongly that if you want to teach mindfulness, it's crucial that it's something that you deeply desire for yourself and your life. If we can be fully present for our students and our colleagues—regardless of the faulty paths we're all on—if we can strive to be attuned and to embody a way of being that is open, curious, kind, and accepting, we can transform our relationships and our schools.

Additional Resources

- "I See You. Everyone Matters," *Greater Good in Education,* https://ggie.berkeley.edu/practice/i-see-you-everyone-matters

- "Practicing Mindfulness in Groups: Nine Activities and Exercises," *PostivePsychology,* https://positivepsychology.com/group-mindfulness-activities

- Cultivating Awareness and Resilience in Education (CARE), https://createforeducation.org/care

- Mindful Schools, https://www.mindfulschools.org

Seeing the Good

The world is full of magic things, patiently waiting for our senses to grow sharper.

—William Butler Yeats

My work has really knocked me off my feet lately, leaving me feeling small, exhausted, unappreciated, helpless, and demoralized. Why? Red tape, bureaucracy, and unwieldy and ineffective communication systems. Of course, I'm not alone. Other educators recently shared the following frustrations with me: "Lack of appreciation." "Parents blaming me for their child's lack of effort." "Evaluations." "Leadership." "Meetings, no time, planning every evening, no parent involvement."

With a whirl of responsibilities to people and paperwork, it can be difficult to break away from one's tunnel vision. When I feel charged up and turned inward, I know it's time to expand my perspective by getting outdoors, exploring my interests, and beholding those things in life that inspire awe. This month, we'll look outward and savor the beauty around us.

Week 9: Cultivating Curiosity

In the 1986 film *Ferris Bueller's Day Off,* a high school economics teacher (played by Ben Stein) stands expressionless at the front of his classroom, lecturing in a nasal, monotone voice. Every few seconds he poses a simple fill-in-the-blank query. "[Blah, blah]… Anyone, anyone?"

The camera flashes to students' blank faces—some of them with mouths agape; some with hateful, disbelieving eyes; and one waking up with a pool of drool on his desk. As a teen, I empathized with the students in that classroom, but I was amused (and then haunted) by this teacher with the life snuffed out of him. The classroom atmosphere was dismal.

Enter my college biology teacher. He was literally gleeful when he talked about insects. At that time, I couldn't have cared less, yet his energy was contagious. His eagerness, his fascination with his subject, and his joyful curiosity lit up that large lecture hall and sparked my own interest.

When it comes to curiosity and your own love of learning, how do you see yourself? Do you feel fiery and passionate about what you teach? Are you fanning a little flame of interest? Or is that fire in you just about dormant?

We want students to be curious, but what about *us?* With all the challenges in the world and your energies at school often channeled to testing, grading, and academic hoop-jumping, how do *you* find joy in learning? You can take advantage of your human capacity for *curiosity* and all the energy, interest, and enjoyment it brings.

A Pathway

Curiosity has multiple dimensions; it isn't a single trait. Instead of asking yourself whether you feel curious these days, why not begin by exploring *how* you are curious. Researcher Todd Kashdan and his team (2018) have identified five specific dimensions of curiosity:

- *"Joyous Exploration" Curiosity:* You are filled with wonder and fascinated by the world—like when you travel to a new place, learn the etymology of a new word, or pursue hobbies like geocaching or stargazing.

- *"Need to Know" Curiosity:* You are driven to seek answers when there is a gap in your knowledge—like when you're prepping for a science lesson, and the robot you built just went belly-up, literally. What do you need to know to fix it? (This dimension is technically called "Deprivation Sensitivity.")

- *"Social" Curiosity:* You want to know more about another person, so you observe them, talk with them—like when you try to find out what makes your new friend laugh or you ask gentle questions of that quiet student, exploring their interests.

- *"Accepting the Anxiety" Curiosity:* You tolerate any uncomfortable feelings that may come with a new experience, and they don't hold you back—like when you unashamedly take up hip hop dancing or race car driving although you've never tried them before. (This dimension is technically called "Stress Tolerance.")

- *"Thrill Seeking" Curiosity:* You take risks because you enjoy new and exciting experiences—like when you topple over desks and transform your history class-room into a "trench warfare" setting or you go snowboarding or waterskiing for the first time. You don't just tolerate the anxiety; it feeds you.

Do you resonate with one or more of these dimensions? If so, you may already be reaping the benefits. If not, there's a lot to look forward to! Researchers link curiosity with intrinsic motivation. Curious people may also be more hopeful and purposeful—with clear long- and short-term goals. And when you meet a goal that is driven by your authentic desire to learn, you may also get a lasting boost in well-being.

Our brain chemistry changes when we become curious, which helps us learn and remember information (Gruber et al. 2014). Research suggests that curious people tend to be more playful, emotionally expressive, non-defensive and non-critical, and tolerant of anxiety (Kashdan et al. 2013; Sheldon et al. 2015). Curiosity appears to be a force that not only enhances learning but also opens us up to more positive perspectives and experiences.

An Action

If you would like to discover which curiosity dimensions best describe you, take Todd Kashdan's survey in Additional Resources. Then, consider a skill or interest you would like to explore. For example, you may want to go to a café to observe the subtle social dynamics at play. Or perhaps you've always wanted to try bungee jumping. Maybe you can't get to Greece this week, but you want to "travel" the streets of Athens using Google Maps' street-view cameras. Carve out some time to pursue a curiosity this week and go for it.

Guiding Questions

After you've explored an interest or tried a new activity, describe how it felt. If you pursued an interest that made you anxious, how did you feel before, during, and after your experience? Or if you were compelled to try a new hobby, what motivated you? How can you draw from this experience to support your students in pursuing their own curiosities? How can you create more freedom for students to *explore*—in the classroom, on the playground, and beyond?

Benefits

Research indicates that the more autonomy and choice you have, the more curious you'll be (Schutte and Malouff 2019). As educators, we can create more spaces in our own lives for joyful exploration. If we spent a little less time running the numbers and a bit more time learning and exploring with our colleagues, wouldn't staff meetings be more engaging? How might a widespread focus on curiosity shift our school climate and energize staff and students?

Louis Pasteur said, "To know how to wonder and question is the first step of the mind toward discovery." If we welcome all types of curiosity in ourselves and our students, we aren't only celebrating the joy of learning but also honoring the unique minds and passions of everyone in our school.

Additional Resources

- "Five-Dimensional Curiosity Scale," https://www.toddkashdan.com/toddkashdan /wp-content/uploads/2018/02/Curiosity-5DC-measure-Kashdan-et-al.-2017.pdf

- Todd Kashdan, *Curious? Discover the Missing Ingredient to a Fulfilling Life*

Week 10: Connecting with the Natural World

I'm feeling a little stir crazy on this winter morning. After spending endless pandemic months indoors, I've become more appreciative of the few moments I spend outside each day. In some ways, this sustained pause (a sort of house arrest) primes me to consider how most of us tend to spend our time—indoors.

Day-to-day stressors propel us from building to building, task to task, as many educators live with an ongoing sense of "time pressure" (Jennings et al. 2013). A global survey tells us that 90 percent of people spend close to twenty-two hours indoors every day; one in six of us almost never goes outside (Westermann 2019).

However, when I pop up from my desk and saunter around the neighborhood for five or ten minutes, I watch an energetic Rottweiler jumping at the chorus of birdsong above him (while his owner hunkers down on his leash). Then I stand under my favorite oak tree and consciously fill my lungs with crisp, fresh air—so sweet.

And I'm not alone in craving time outside. Other educational professionals shared with me: "I'd be lost if I didn't get outside with nature." "The outdoors keep me grounded and present—especially on weekends when I'm trying to recharge." "This is my top tip to all of my teachers in order to avoid burnout—get out in nature daily."

A Pathway

What happens in our brains when we connect with nature? Stanford researchers found no changes in brain activity when study participants walked in an urban setting, yet walking through natural settings demonstrated decreased activity in an area of the prefrontal cortex associated with self-focus and rumination (Bratman et al. 2015a). In another study, participants with mobile EEG recorders passing through three different areas (two urban and one green) demonstrated lower frustration, arousal, and engagement, and higher "meditation" when they moved into the green space, and the EEG recorders indicated higher engagement when they left green spaces (Aspinall et al. 2015). In other words, EEG evidence pointed to greater relaxation in nature.

Apparently, when we connect with nature, shifts in our attention seem to help us to recharge. Because we may be "on alert" in urban environments (e.g., with the intense pace of life, the crowds, the need to avoid cars that might hit us), researchers are finding that exposure to nature seems to draw on a different form of attention. Natural environments offer us appealing sensory stimuli (fragrant plants, soothing landscapes, gurgling streams) that gently draw our attention in a "bottom-up" fashion, so that our more immediate, direct "top-down" capacity for attention can rest a bit. When we take a break from the more urgent aspects of day-to-day life that require focus, we can reboot so that we become more consciously and strategically attentive (Berman et al. 2008).

Research also suggests that new teachers' experiences in nature influence the value they place on *student* learning in nature (Blatt and Patrick 2014). In other words, your outdoor time (even as a child) may influence your instructional planning. How much do you value time in nature? And what role does nature play in your students' lives at school?

To be honest, as a suburban kid now living in a semi-urban setting, I've been hesitant to take my students (children, teens, and adults) outside, because I feared their restlessness and distraction. Yet some of the leading researchers in the field tell a different story about how nature can enhance student learning. In one experimental study, Min Kuo and her team (2018) found that teachers experienced greater student engagement outdoors with fewer "redirects" needed (stopping instruction to draw students' attention back to a learning task).

Time outdoors can also enhance students' social and emotional well-being. For example, students who experienced lower self-esteem and felt marginalized at school reported statistically significant changes in self-concept—along with benefits to emotional regulation, group cohesion, and trust—after participating in an outdoor education program (White 2012).

Based on a more extensive review of studies, Kuo and her colleagues (2019) suggest that nature provides a quieter and calmer context for learning that seems to lower stress and improve attention while also potentially enhancing enjoyment and interest in learning.

An Action

Time in nature can improve our health and happiness (Richardson et al. 2016). Walking in a forested environment can promote relaxation by engaging your parasympathetic system (the calming rest-and-digest system) and suppressing your sympathetic (fight-or-flight) system (J. Lee et al. 2014).

So I invite you to spend some time, if possible, in a forest (or near trees and plants). Slow down and pay attention to your sensory experience. You might focus on identifying all the sounds you hear (including silence), notice all the colors and shapes around you, or take deep breaths to savor the scents of the trees and plants.

Guiding Questions

What do you see, hear, feel, smell, or even taste in the air? What do you notice about yourself while you are in this space? Do you experience any physiological changes? What do you notice in yourself *after* your time outdoors? Is it possible to prioritize a few more minutes a day outside? How and where might you go?

Benefits

Is connecting with nature a fundamental psychological need? Research tells us that humans (regardless of culture, age, and socioeconomic status) benefit from time in nature as a counter to more urbanized environments. With over half of the globe living in urban areas, studies show that our exposure to nature can potentially bolster our mental health and psychological functioning (Bratman et al. 2015b).

In fact, walking in nature, visiting a natural environment—or even viewing pictures of nature—may yield both cognitive *and* affective benefits (Berman et al. 2008; Bratman et al. 2015b). For example, people taking a fifty-minute walk in nature (versus an urban environment) demonstrated increased working memory as well as a decrease in anxiety, rumination, and negative feelings.

And if you happen to live in a busy, bustling city, even a brief visit to a natural environment, like an urban park or the woods, can relieve stress. Researchers in Finland found that participants spending time in green spaces experienced a decrease in stress (measured by cortisol levels). And the greener, the better. People in that study who spent time in a more wild wooded area reported that it was more restorative even after the experiment concluded (Tyrväinen et al. 2013).

Students and teachers—all of us—can both restore, reboot, and reenergize with a little more time in the natural world. It's often the simple things around us that call us back to awareness and aliveness—the deep pull of the ocean, the gentle whisper of the breeze, the icy gleam of the moon. My favorite poet, Mary Oliver, reminds us, "To pay attention, this is our endless and proper work."

Additional Resources

- "Noticing Nature," *Greater Good in Action,* https://ggia.berkeley.edu/practice/noticing_nature

- "What Happens When We Reconnect with Nature," *Greater Good,* https://greatergood.berkeley.edu/article/item/what_happens_when_we_reconnect_with_nature

- "The 'Indoor Generation' and the Health Risks of Spending More Time Inside," *USA Today,* https://www.usatoday.com/story/sponsor-story/velux/2018/05/15/indoor-generation-and-health-risks-spending-more-time-inside/610289002

Week 11: Appreciating Beauty

A passage from Toni Morrison's *The Bluest Eye* registered vividly when I first read it in college—and I've returned to it many times throughout the years. Pecola Breedlove is a young Black girl who longs for recognition—who wants to be seen as good and beautiful in a world that "stood astride her ugliness": "Pecola stood a little apart from us…. She seemed to fold into herself, like a pleated wing…. I wanted to open her up, crisp her edges, ram a stick down that hunched and curving spine, force her to stand erect and spit the misery out on the streets. But she held it in where it could lap up into her eyes."

This book, this scene, this moment continues to gnaw at me—as a blue-eyed blonde—even more than a powerful "discussion" or "policy debate" about racial justice. This is the power of art—it can rouse our hearts more deeply, more viscerally. It can humanize and connect us. In the real world, however, we don't always "see" or feel in this way. Many of us move through life at a steady clip—often bypassing opportunities for affinity and relationship. As an educator-human, I am aware of the dangers of overlooking—of missing—what is right in front of me. How can we learn to *see*—by knowing the facts or contemplating our experience?

A Pathway

Consider the word "contemplation," which means "to mark out a space for observation." Researcher and author Arthur Zajoncs (2016) distinguishes *knowing* from *contemplation.* Basic *knowing* (comprehension) reflects an early stage of learning while deep, *contemplative engagement,* over time, can lead to a more fully integrated, internalized education.

Because we live in a rational world, we're more likely to be disconnected from our body, senses, and environment. However, when we slow down and take time to focus on others—both objects and people—we are engaging in what psychologist Mark Freeman (2015) calls an "ethics of attention," in which we detach from our egos and engage in a more holistic, experiential approach to learning and understanding—which can lead to personal growth.

What might this look like? Consider the contemplative practice called "beholding." Beholding, as an exercise, draws on our sense of sight to enrich our engagement with an object over time and can slowly shift the way we see the world and ourselves.

One of my favorite stories of "beholding" from the Center of Contemplative Mind in Society features Professor Joanna Ziegler, who took her students to the Worcester Art Museum every week for an entire semester. Each week she asked her class to sit in front of the same painting and to answer the same, simple question: "What do you see?" (See Additional Resources.)

Students learned to navigate their distracted minds and to repeatedly bring their attention back to that painting—for thirteen weeks in a row! Ziegler says that her students' perspectives shifted from hate to love as they began to experience a form of reverence for that painting. Over time, they learned to let go of their preoccupations, preconceptions, and biases and to observe, "see," and "behold" that work of art. Most importantly, she discovered that students' attentiveness transformed into a deeper sense of care for that piece of art. Ziegler believes that *care* is "the foundation of moral concern."

An Action

This week, choose a piece of art (a painting or sculpture), an object in nature (a plant, tree, or flower), or a photograph of someone's face or a natural landscape, and take a few minutes each day to slow down and really look at it. Each day, ask yourself, *What do I see?*

Guiding Questions

How does your appreciation of this object or piece of art shift and change throughout the week? Describe your experience of "beholding."

Benefits

Now that you have engaged in "beholding" as one form of contemplative practice, it's worth considering how contemplative activities might enhance your students' and colleagues' day-to-day learning. Contemplative education features activities and practices that enhance our awareness of ourselves and our connection to the world (Jennings 2008).

Activities in which you sustain your attention, like yoga and mindfulness practices, affect brain structures associated with emotion regulation and cognitive control, including executive functions like working memory, impulse control, and cause-and-effect thinking. When you engage in contemplative practices, you're likely to experience less stress, greater self-awareness, improved self-regulation, and even enhanced empathy and compassion (Roeser and Zelazo 2012; Shapiro et al. 2015).

Pre-service teachers who participated in contemplative exercises as a regular part of their coursework acknowledged the value of "surrendering to curiosity" through group contemplation. They appreciated the opportunities to engage in a slowed-down, unforced dialogue that is inclusive, supportive, and collaborative—where everyone contributes to a shared understanding (Pelech and Kelly 2017).

The more I engage in practices like these, I feel more settled into myself, and more aware and attuned to the world around me. No doubt Henry David Thoreau understood the time and patience invested in deeply *seeing* when he said, "Wisdom does not inspect, but behold. We must look a long time before we can see." I want to really see and be alive to this world. I want to see my students. I want my students to be seen.

I think Toni Morrison's rendering of Pecola Breedlove in *The Bluest Eye* planted a seed in me as a college student. As a reader, I beheld her, and still do, seeing the good in her that many characters in the novel did not. Professor Joanna Ziegler believes that when we practice *beholding,* we grow the capacity to focus on what's valuable in art, nature, and life: "This is the foundation of an ethical awareness, the beginning of an ethical stance."

Additional Resources

- "Beholding," *The Center for Contemplative Mind in Society,* https://www .contemplativemind.org/practices/tree/beholding

- "Contemplation and Creativity," *Greater Good in Education,* https://ggie.berkeley .edu/collection/contemplation-and-creativity

- "Mindful Seeing for Elementary Students," *Greater Good in Education,* https:// ggie.berkeley.edu/practice/mindful-seeing-for-elementary-students

Week 12: Discovering Awe

Last night's Netflix experience offered me the shift in perspective I needed during a head-down, in-the-weeds, inwardly focused time at work.

Have you seen the 2020 documentary *My Octopus Teacher?* Burned out and emotionally exhausted, filmmaker Craig Foster finds himself drawn to the ocean, where he ends up spending almost a year visiting and befriending an octopus. He begins his year snorkeling through a sea forest just off the Western Cape of South Africa—and that's where he meets her, the octopus, and becomes mesmerized. He is fascinated by her intelligence, her vulnerability, her intricate defense system, and her resilience. At the end of that year of devotion, he finds himself more alive to the world and more "sensitized" and attuned to others, including his son.

You may not have time to glory in a kelp forest and befriend a sea creature, but how often do you take time to look beyond your immediate experience—to consider the deep expanse of the ocean? The inestimable speed of light? The possibility of life on other planets?

A Pathway

"Awe is the feeling of being in the presence of something vast that transcends your understanding of the world," says researcher Dacher Keltner (2016b). When you feel awe, you sense yourself as part of a much larger and more complex reality (Chen and Mongrain 2020). Psychologists also tell us that awe is an emotional response that may make you more aware of the gaps in your knowledge (McPhetres 2019), which can feed your curiosity and interest.

When you witness something "awesome," you are also more likely to see yourself in "collectivist terms" (Shiota et al. 2007). In other words, you more readily identify yourself as a member of culture, community, or a greater cause. Or, as Craig Foster expressed in *My Octopus Teacher,* you feel like you are "part of this world—and not a visitor."

With all this in mind, you may wonder what typically stirs up awe. When researcher Michelle Shiota and her team (2007) asked university students, they frequently described being in nature or engaging with art or music. Even great acts of "skill" or "virtue" can elicit awe (Keltner 2016b). For example, activities like hiking near a waterfall, visiting a museum, or attending a rock concert may leave you awestruck. Or you may find yourself captivated by the work of an architect, an inventor, or even an activist.

More recent research suggests that we don't necessarily have to be in the presence of something (like nature or art) to experience awe. In fact, we can nurture awe through our own imagination, as well as our memory (Chen and Mongrain 2020). Can you recall a time when you saw something that astonished you—or filled you with a sense of wonder (like camping under the stars or looking out of an airplane window)? Or do you ever imagine what it was like for a scientist or mathematician to come up with that groundbreaking theory or magical formula?

An Action

Researcher Dacher Keltner (2016b) suggests awe as a "prescription" for daily well-being. Each day this week, take a few moments to experience awe. Here are a few suggestions:

- Watch an awe-inspiring video featuring art, music, or a sweeping landscape (e.g., Colossal Art [https://www.thisiscolossal.com/] or the docuseries *Planet Earth* [https://www.bbc.co.uk/programmes/b006mywy].

- Spend a few minutes writing about an experience that inspired awe in you.

- If possible, take a short walk through your neighborhood and notice (with all your senses) the trees, the plants, or the imposing buildings above you (if you are in a city). Open yourself up to experiencing the vastness around you.

Guiding Questions

Now, pull out your journal and respond to the following: What do you sense in yourself while you engage in these activities? Do you feel shifts in your body? Does your posture change? What feelings come up for you? What sorts of thoughts or wonderings fill your mind? Do you feel more connected to others? More creative? More curious?

Benefits

Initial research indicates that awe may be good for both our minds and our bodies. Studies link awe with a more positive mood, a stronger sense of connectedness, and increases in critical, creative, and flexible thinking (S. Allen 2018a; Chirico et al. 2018), as well as reduced inflammation, which can be predictive of a stronger immune response (Stellar et al. 2015).

Awe may even benefit our relationships. When you reflect on something bigger, more powerful and awesome, you're less likely to focus on yourself and more likely to reach out to help others. Studies show that people feeling awe behaved with greater generosity, helping behavior, and "prosocial emotions" like compassion when compared to others (Piff et al. 2015).

Now that you've experienced a daily dose of awe, it's also worth considering how students experience awe. No doubt you can recall a toddler captivated by the newly fallen snow or a small child absorbed by an ant colony. What happens to children's capacity for awe as they begin school? Kieran Egan (2014) suggests ways to keep students' minds "awake and alive" in the classroom. We can make genuine questions and inquiry central to learning; we can celebrate stories "with transcendent qualities"—where the main character displays a virtue in overcoming a challenge—or we can take a familiar object like a stick or a flower and see it with fresh eyes.

Perhaps all we need are a few prompts to open ourselves up to the astonishing world around us. Years ago, soon after my grandfather died, I had a dream where he told me, "Amy, you need to look up" (both literally and figuratively, I think). He told me that I spent too much time hunkered down, tending my own thoughts—that there was so much more to see and do. He was right.

Experiences of awe help us look up and see beyond our immediate experience. Despite the suffering in the world, there's always beauty to behold. Look up. Look around. See the good—and share it with others.

Additional Resources

- "Eight Reasons Why Awe Makes Your Life Better," *Greater Good,* https://greatergood.berkeley.edu/article/item/eight_reasons_why_awe_makes_your_life_better

- "What Is Awe?," *Greater Good,* https://greatergood.berkeley.edu/topic/awe/definition

Embracing the Good

When you are grateful, your heart is open—open towards others, open for surprise.

—David Steindl-Rast

As teachers, we're told to leave our problems at the door of the classroom so we can focus on our students. Perhaps you try, but if you're like me, you have a shadow side grappling with everything on your figurative plate—from personal insecurities to daily stressors to larger institutional inequities. Although we've been taking time to recognize the good around us, defaulting to false positivity can also backfire.

We don't need to be disingenuous about the challenges we face; we can entertain and hold both realities. There is suffering, *and* there is good in the world. During difficult times, sharing, embracing, and anticipating goodness through gratitude, forgiveness, and good wishes can help to restore our sense of connectedness to others and feed a more authentic sense of optimism.

Week 13: Prioritizing Gratitude

Author Glennon Doyle reminds us that the world is brutal, but it's also beautiful. In fact, it's "brutiful." This morning I write, heavy with grief. It's the two-year anniversary of my best friend Lisa's death from breast cancer. I'd prefer to curl up under the covers, and yet there is a hummingbird with a beautiful scarlet neck on a wire just outside my window as I type. It's fairy-like, magical—a reminder of the joy Lisa and I shared and a sign of promise.

When times are tough, there's no better antidote than opening ourselves to gratitude. We can hold both our grief and our joyfulness, though it sometimes takes courage to focus on the good.

A Pathway

Robert Emmons (2007), perhaps the world's leading scientific expert on gratitude, argues that gratitude has two key components. First, gratitude is "an affirmation of goodness." There's so much suffering in this world, but gratitude tells us there's also a lot of good—and we get to experience that good. Second, gratitude is "a recognition that sources of this goodness are outside of ourselves." Others (or a higher power, if one is spiritually inclined) help us to experience the goodness in our lives.

Gratitude, as a social emotion, is a powerful ingredient of health and well-being for both individuals and communities. It can strengthen relationships, because it compels us to acknowledge how we've been supported or affirmed by others. Imagine what gratitude can do to build community in our schools—and to cultivate a sense of belonging.

What can this look like for you, your colleagues, and your students? Perhaps you choose to regularly participate in staff "gratitude circles." Or you offer ongoing opportunities to honor and appreciate students in your classroom. You can also incorporate individual reflection activities into staff and classroom meetings. (See Additional Resources below for more specific gratitude practices.)

An Action

This week, write a letter of gratitude to someone you appreciate—and *deliver it personally* (on the phone or via Zoom, if needed). If possible, read it out loud.

Guiding Questions

Reflect on the experience in your journal. How did you feel when you wrote the letter? What was it like to read it aloud? How did the recipient respond?

Benefits

Studies indicate that gratitude practices like counting your blessings or writing about things you are grateful for can improve your physical and mental health—and enhance your willingness to trust others (Chan 2010; Seligman et al. 2005). School leaders who wrote gratitude letters expressed more motivation to invest in their professional relationships and received gratitude from staff and students—a ripple effect of appreciation (Waters and Stokes 2015). When gratitude becomes part of your workplace culture, you're also likely to feel better about your job.

In fact, we're learning that teachers who regularly practice gratitude are less likely to experience two aspects of burnout—emotional exhaustion and depersonalization; instead, they tend to have a greater sense of meaning, personal accomplishment, and happiness in their lives (Waters 2012). And in a smaller study, pre-service teachers who focused on gratitude during their internships reported improved relationships, a greater sense of well-being, and better teaching outcomes (Howells and Cumming 2012).

Further, when students practice gratitude, they can experience an increase in connectedness, satisfaction with school, and engagement in learning—as well as less stress and depression (Jin and Wang 2019; Bono et al. 2020). In fact, a recent study tells us that students' gratitude for their teachers seems to serve as a resource in facing personal challenges outside of school (Liauw et al. 2018).

Considering these findings, gratitude isn't trite at all—even in the worst of times. One of the greatest privileges of my life was to sit next to my best friend's bed with my laptop as she dictated letters of love and appreciation to her husband and her two boys. I still look back on those moments as deeply sacred. We exchanged our own gratitude letters that day as well—just two months before her death.

There is nothing more precious than acknowledging those people in your life who support you in big and small ways. With gratitude, we celebrate the good that connects and sustains us.

Additional Resources

- "Gratitude for Adults," *Greater Good in Education,* https://ggie.berkeley.edu /my-well-being/gratitude-for-adults/#tab__3

- "Gratitude for Students," *Greater Good in Education,* https://ggie.berkeley.edu /student-well-being/gratitude-for-students/#tab__3

- "What Teens Are Thankful For," *Greater Good,* https://greatergood.berkeley .edu/video/item/what_teens_are_actually_thankful_for

Week 14: Learning to Forgive

As a teacher, I find that compassion and empathy come to me naturally, but with forgiveness, I struggle. I've stewed with resentment over conflicts with colleagues and wallowed in woundedness when family members rejected me. I've suffered for hours, days, and even years. Maybe you can relate?

The problem is that without forgiveness—letting go—we hold our feelings of abandonment, disappointment, and anger in our minds and bodies. The result is stress. When we ruminate, turning things over and over in our minds, we can also experience increased muscle tension, spikes in blood pressure, heart rate variability, and increases in cortisol production, which is a chemical marker of stress (McCullough et al. 2007).

Forgiveness expert Fred Luskin's words provide some perspective on how to get out of the figurative pit. "Forgiveness is the ability to make peace with the word 'no.'" Maybe your parents aren't there for you, your partner has betrayed you, or your colleague resists all your efforts to collaborate. For whatever reason, you aren't getting what you want. Luskin claims that when we forgive, we have the resilience to "be at peace with 'no'" and to go on to live our life with a willingness to "give the next moment a chance."

I love this; it's beautiful. But it's still difficult to let go.

A Pathway

Perhaps we can begin with a better understanding of forgiveness and what it entails. Researcher Everett Worthington (2020) identifies two types of forgiveness. "Decisional forgiveness" involves choosing to let go of anger and resentment toward someone who wronged you in some way (e.g., *I choose to forgive that student for all the hateful insults they hurled at me in class*). "Emotional forgiveness," on the other hand, draws on compassion, sympathy, or empathy as tools for replacing negative emotions with positive ones (e.g., *My ego hurts, and I'm angry that my efforts go unnoticed, but this person is going through a lot; they are scared and tired and sad and probably feel vulnerable right now*). It is one thing to choose forgiveness; it is another to unearth all the messy feelings around it. While decisional forgiveness can help us begin to repair and heal relationships, the best way to reduce stress is to forgive on an emotional level.

With over one hundred forgiveness intervention studies to date (Worthington 2020), we know that forgiveness is a trainable skill, but it's also a nuanced process that doesn't typically happen in an instant. If you're looking for more concrete direction on how to begin the journey, Everett Worthington's five-step REACH plan is one of the most studied forgiveness frameworks (see Additional Resources). He developed a workbook that walks you through each of following components (Recall, Empathize, Altruism, Commit, and Hold on):

- *R*ecall the hurt. Describe it as objectively as you can.

- *E*mpathize. Focus on understanding the feelings of the person who wronged you.

- *A*ltruism. Consider a time you hurt someone and were forgiven. Then, decide to offer the same gift to the person who just hurt you.

- *C*ommit. Own your decision by choosing to forgive that person publicly or in a way that makes it real for you.

- *H*old on. You may not forget the hurt, but you can remind yourself of your choice to forgive.

With these steps in mind, it's important to remember that you may not fully reverse course toward forgiveness. Everett Worthington says that whether we experience "transformation" or "gradual change," the goal here is to "change direction." One study of teachers revealed that it's particularly challenging to forgive when you perceive the wrong committed was "intentional" (Nasser and Abu-Nimer 2012).

An Action

Research suggests that you can do three things to prepare to forgive someone (Worthington 2020). First, recall the wrongdoing as objectively as you can. Next, try to understand the perspective of the person who hurt you. Finally, consider a time you hurt someone, and they forgave you. How did that feel? Can you offer that same gift to someone else this week?

Guiding Questions

What happened as you completed the three steps above? Were you able to offer someone forgiveness? Why or why not? How does your empathy and compassion play a role in your ability to forgive "emotionally"?

Benefits

When we learn to forgive on an emotional level, we let go of obsessive thinking, potentially lessen anxiety and depression, and experience other benefits like stronger immune systems and healthier hearts (McCullough et al. 2007). Forgiveness doesn't just yield individual benefits; it can also transform communities and workplaces—maybe even schools (Nasser and Abu-Nimer 2012).

Over the past several years, researchers like Bob Enright have been studying forgiveness interventions for children. In one fascinating study, Iranian eighth graders from different ethnic groups who participated in a forgiveness-education program not only reported a stronger tendency to forgive, but they also experienced less anger and less ethnic prejudice (Ghobari Bonab et al. 2020).

We're also learning that when teachers participate in mindfulness programs that focus on developing prosocial skills like empathy and compassion, they are more likely and capable of forgiving students and colleagues—even in the following school year (S. S. Braun et al. 2020). This makes sense to me, because mindfulness is a practice of openness and acceptance (of your own experience and life circumstances). If we can extend that same openness and acceptance to others, perhaps we can all live more peacefully.

So I'm learning to be at peace with "no" by drawing on my capacity to be empathic and compassionate. I'm also learning that forgiveness is a way of being in the world. As Martin Luther King Jr. reminds us: it's a "constant attitude," not an "occasional act."

Additional Resources

- "What Is Forgiveness?," *Greater Good,* https://greatergood.berkeley.edu/topic/forgiveness/definition

- "Your Path to REACH Forgiveness: Become a More Forgiving Person in Less Than Two Hours," http://www.evworthington-forgiveness.com/diy-workbooks

- Fred Luskin, *Forgive for Good: A Proven Prescription for Health and Happiness*

Week 15: Sending Good Wishes to Others

Do you ever wake up with a feeling of dread?

At one point in my teaching career, I worked in a very toxic setting. It didn't start that way, but when a new administrator took over, I watched the climate shift dramatically. My colleagues began to close their office doors, and I often sat through staff meetings with mild nausea.

For months, I woke up with a sense of heaviness and dread. I loved teaching, and I loved my students, but I had to work up the courage to literally step out of the car, walk toward my building, open the door, and hit those hallways every day.

Teacher burnout and demoralization are real for many of us—whether we're facing increasing demands on our time and energy, a lack of support from leadership, or barriers to the resources we need to do our best work. This can undermine our health as well as our ability to connect with our students.

A Pathway

Here's one simple way I redirected my focus and found comfort and purpose—even on the toughest days. I pulled into the parking lot, paused, gazed at the school building, and mentally sent good wishes to myself, my students, and my colleagues: "May I (and you) be safe; may I (you) be happy; may I (you) be healthy; may I (you) live with ease." Because I started my mornings this way, I found that the kind sentiments quietly infused themselves into many of my daily interactions, bolstering me emotionally as I confronted the more difficult aspects of the job.

What was I doing? I was engaging in an abbreviated form of a "loving-kindness" practice in which you extend feelings of warmth and care toward yourself, a close person, a neutral person, a difficult person, and a stranger.

As I look back on this morning ritual, I realize how it moved me from a helpless, disempowered feeling to one of focus, care, and even I-can-do-this agency. Sending good thoughts to everyone in that building, including colleagues who confounded and frustrated me, was a challenge, but an exercise in personal growth. It made me feel more purposeful and more in control of my life. Now I have a better understanding of why. When we focus on sending kindness or warm wishes to others, we are engaging in a compassion practice. Researchers describe compassion as both *concern* for another's suffering along with a *desire to help* alleviate that suffering (Goetz et al. 2010). Compassion can bolster resilience and improve our relationships, and it's also associated with more satisfaction and growth in friendships, making us less vindictive toward others (Condon and DeSteno 2011; Shonin et al. 2015).

At the same time, empathy and compassion have their limits. In *The Power Paradox*, psychologist Dacher Keltner (2016a) reviews multiple studies suggesting that with more power, our capacity for empathy and compassion declines. So it may be helpful to map out the power structures in our schools and to consider how they might influence or limit opportunities for empathy, compassion, and connection.

The good news is that compassion workshops, programs, and trainings abound for both teachers and students, and researchers have reviewed programs that have been adapted for students and schools. We are learning that children's ability to be compassionate grows as they develop the ability to regulate their emotions and take others' perspectives (Lavelle Heineberg 2016).

We are also learning that "mindful teaching" is not just about a teacher's ability to be present and aware, but it's also very much about compassion—extending it to yourself and to your students and colleagues.

An Action

When you arrive at school each morning, mentally send good wishes to yourself and a student or colleague: "May I (you) be safe; may I (you) be happy; may I (you) be healthy; may I (you) live with ease."

Guiding Questions

How did this practice affect your well-being this week? Did you sense changes in yourself? If so, describe them.

What emotions arose for you during this practice? Did you find yourself struggling (or even resisting) to wish particular people well? If so, acknowledge that. This is a practice, and you can't force good feelings. Just showing up and trying is a great first step.

Benefits

A recent review of compassion studies with adults tells us that regularly practicing compassion can increase our self-compassion—or kindness toward ourselves—and our overall well-being while reducing depression, anxiety, and psychological distress (Kirby et al. 2017).

More specifically, student-teachers who practiced loving-kindness reported higher levels of empathy and lower levels of stress (Csaszar et al. 2018).

And in another study of loving-kindness practice (Kang et al. 2014), adult participants experienced a reduction in implicit attitudes or biases against traditionally stigmatized groups after only six weeks of practice. In other words, regularly sending good wishes to others may help us to become more understanding, open-minded, and accepting of others. The Dalai Lama sums up these benefits more simply: "If you want others to be happy, practice compassion. If you want to be happy, practice compassion."

Additional Resources

- Dacher Keltner, *The Power Paradox: How We Gain and Lose Influence*

- "Train Your Brain to Be Kinder," *Greater Good,* https://greatergood.berkeley.edu /video/item/train_your_brain_to_be_kinder

- "About Compassion Training," *The Center for Compassion and Altruism Research and Education at Stanford University,* http://ccare.stanford.edu/education/about -compassion-training

---

Week 16: Choosing Optimism

"Sometimes she just seems *too* happy," said an anonymous student on my teacher feed-back form. I often joke with other teachers about this critique, but it still gnaws at me a bit. "Enthusiastic" is probably the word most students use to describe me as a teacher, and yet this comment suggests I may "put it on" a little too much at times. The truth is, my teaching persona is quite different from my at-home self. I'm a total extrovert as a teacher, but an introvert at home. I'm positive and joyful in class, and I'm often quiet, introspective, and a bit more cynical about life with my trusted loved ones. In fact, I grew up in a glass-half-empty home where negativity ruled over positivity.

I remember how relieved I was to learn of our "negativity bias" as humans (Hanson and Mendius 2009). We're wired to respond to perceived threats (physical or psychological). These days we aren't literally running from predators, yet we're bombarded with all kinds of psychological threats, big and small (your students tell you that you're a "bad teacher" or your colleagues sigh when you stand up to speak at staff meetings). No wonder we feel charged-up, defensive, and negative. Our physiological defense system fires up to protect us. If we're designed to spot and remember the negative, how do we hold on to the positive?

A Pathway

Multiple studies suggest that your "positivity ratio"—the balance of your positive to negative emotions—can be linked to your well-being. According to psychologists Barbara Fredrickson and Marcial Losada (2005), if you experience about three positive emotions for every negative emotion, you're more likely to flourish, experiencing positive mental health characterized by goodness, growth, and resilience. Although researchers still debate whether 2.9 to 1 (to be exact) is the critical ratio in question, many psychologists agree with the basic idea.

Of course, Western cultures—and Americans in particular—tend to glorify optimism and enthusiasm, so there's a caveat to note here. Psychologist Susan David (2016) surveyed seventy thousand adults and found that one-third of us either judge ourselves for having "bad" emotions like anger or sadness, or we push our "negative" emotions away. The thing is, all emotions are potential tools and teachers. If we deny uncomfortable emotions in favor of false positivity, we aren't fully living, and we aren't necessarily learning how to navigate the tough stuff. So if we choose to focus on the good, that doesn't mean that we must ignore or suppress the bad.

When we share our optimism as teachers, however, we *can* shift the dynamic in our classrooms. Researchers are discovering how teachers use optimism as an "instructional resource." When Tanya Vehkakoski (2020) analyzed recorded lessons by special-education teachers, she discovered four ways teachers boosted student optimism around learning. They encouraged students to see the positive by reframing students' statements, they praised students' earlier actions, they provided inspiring examples of peer successes, and they offered additional instructional support as students worked through problems.

An Action

If you'd like to practice optimism in an authentic way, here is one simple practice to try this week. Adults who participated in this activity every night for seven days reported less pessimism and emotional exhaustion one month later (Littman-Ovadia and Nir 2014). Every night before you go to sleep, write down three things (items, people, or events) you look forward to the next day. For example, last night I wrote: "My morning cup of tea, quiet time to write, and my small-group teaching session."

Guiding Questions

Throughout the week, take note of what it feels like to anticipate the good things ahead of you. Did you find yourself more appreciative of particular people or experiences the following day? Do you see yourself channeling more positive energy in your classroom? If so, how?

At the end of the week, reflect on the overall experience. Did you notice a shift in your energy, emotions, or stress level? Describe what you observed in yourself.

Benefits

Positive emotions like joy, excitement, and hope contribute to our overall happiness and can have a "broadening effect" in our lives. Counter to our automatic responses to threat, they open us up to creativity, flexibility, and new ways of acting and thinking. And when we broaden our perspective, we tend to become more resourceful and resilient. When we feel better, we cope better (Fredrickson 2001).

This research applies to teachers, too. In one study, teachers with a higher ratio of positive to negative emotions reported more engagement, purpose, and personal growth in their work—as well as greater self-acceptance and positive relationships (Rusu and Colomeischi 2020). In another study of pre-service teachers, researchers identified a strong relationship between new teachers' self-efficacy and optimism about their careers (McLennan et al. 2017). This research suggests that if we experience small teaching and learning successes and actively acknowledge them, we may be more likely to generate greater optimism over time. And it's also likely that our optimism reciprocally feeds our belief in ourselves as teachers.

If teacher optimism can positively influence students' capacity for learning, what role does student optimism play? One group of researchers found that students (ages twelve to fifteen) with a high ratio of positive to negative emotions reported higher self-control skills (the ability to meet personal goals, overcome difficulties, delay gratification, cope with psychological distress, etc.), and these skills also seemed to be bolstered by the support of parents and peers (Orkibi et al. 2018). All this evidence points to the power of appreciating the good as we experience it.

Additional Resources

- Susan David, "False Positive Emotions," https://www.youtube.com/watch?v=piRqRnAdcNk

- Barbara Fredrickson, *Positivity: Top-Notch Research Reveals the 3-to-1 Ratio That Will Change Your Life*

Developing Resilience

You may not control all the events that happen to you, but you can decide not to be reduced by them.

—Maya Angelou

We know that simple awareness of our thoughts and feelings is key to living a happier life. Yet it's difficult to float through life with calm, benign detachment when you're weighed down by stress. Yes, we can strive to celebrate the good things, but bad things happen, too—all the time.

The real work occurs as we navigate our conflicting thoughts and feelings about events in our lives. Did that parent actually say *that?* What does this mean about *me?* How *should* I be reacting? Our internal messaging systems—flooded with a range of beliefs, worries, and self-criticism—can gnaw away at our potential for resilience and growth.

As we get to know and understand the thoughts and beliefs that influence our behaviors, we begin to tweak them and develop a kinder, more self-compassionate approach to the way we do life.

Week 17: Identifying Your Beliefs about Emotions

When you were a child, what messages did you receive about emotions? For example, were you taught to believe that emotions are "bad"? If so, to what degree? Some research suggests that believing emotions are completely "uncontrollable" may lead to depressive symptoms. And believing that emotions are bad, in general, can predict poorer psychological health (Ford and Gross 2019). We all grew up in different families and cultures. No doubt our upbringings influenced our beliefs about our emotions quite profoundly.

Now that I study the science of emotions, I can see that the "messages" I received about emotions (and emotional expression) were subtle. No one told me not to cry or yell, but I grew up as the eldest daughter of a minister, and I learned to maintain a cheerful smile and demeanor—especially in public. I carried this sense of duty to the family image everywhere I went.

I vividly remember an argument at the family dinner table interrupted by a phone call from one of my dad's parishioners. Dad jumped from the kitchen table to the phone and shifted his tone from angry to affable in a millisecond. No doubt, we humans follow social norms of politeness and pleasantry, but this moment infused itself into my teen brain. At the time I decided that our family was a bunch of performers—faking our way through life. The implicit message: "Don't let them know that we struggle, too."

But I also now know more about "emotional labor." It takes a lot of effort to adjust your body language, tone, and facial expressions to appear suitable and appropriate. In this case, you may be hiding things you feel or pretending to feel things you don't. Faking it can take a toll on our bodies and minds, leading to a sense of inauthenticity, stress, and burnout (Hochschild 1983).

A Pathway

How do we reconcile our cultural training about "proper" emotional expression with what we're really feeling every day?

Here's an interesting theory to consider. Researcher Jeanne Tsai (2017) has studied the relationship between our ideal versus our *real* emotions. Her research suggests that what *we want to feel* (our ideal affect) often differs from what we feel (our *real* affect). Our culture or upbringing influences what we want to feel, yet our real feelings tend to be more a result of our temperament or personality.

For example, my minister father grew up in a stiff-upper-lip, British, and highly religious culture, so he learned not only that he must *suppress* his anger but also that his anger was a *sin*. Yet he experienced a lot of anger and frustration as a child and teen. His family and culture valued calm and quiet, but his mind and body didn't always feel calm or quiet. When the cultural ideal (suppression of feelings) and the real (expression of feelings) clash within us, we can experience an increase in anxiety or depression as a result (Tsai 2017).

This conflict between the ideal and the real can also play out in our relationships at school. For example, your student's or colleague's real, in-the-moment emotional expression might differ from the form of emotional expression you personally idealize—or what you have been taught to value. Or perhaps your co-teacher rarely speaks directly about their emotions, but you've learned that it's important to openly express—and even describe or label your emotions.

Alternatively, we can also perceive an "ideal affect match" with someone else. For example, if you value calmer, more relaxed emotional expressions (rather than big, toothy, eager smiles), you might be drawn to the sense of calm mirrored in someone else's face. According to the research, you may be more likely to not only find that person more trustworthy, but you may also act more generously toward that person (Park et al. 2017).

And let's take this one step further. Consider how you might subconsciously perpetuate your own cultural preferences for emotional expression as you work with students and colleagues. You might gravitate toward students who demonstrate high-intensity positive emotions—like laughter, extroversion, big and open smiles—or students who demonstrate calm, quiet smiles.

Bottom line: your *ideal* affect (your *beliefs* about emotions) may be more malleable than your *actual* affect. So it's possible to shift your beliefs.

When we think about cultural influences on values and beliefs, it's tricky to draw conclusions about a given culture. So much variation exists across countries, cultures, and contexts—and "essentializing" or "stereotyping" another culture is a dangerous business. Nevertheless, some researchers study cultural differences in emotional expression to help us to move beyond the oversimplified findings out there based on non-diverse participant samples (i.e., the white Western perspective in the United States).

Here are a few of the differences recent research findings identify. Maya Tamir and her colleagues (2015) surveyed over two thousand people across eight countries and found that people tend to want to feel emotions consistent with their values. For example, people who value openness to change also want to feel excitement and interest, whereas people who value conservation want to feel calmer and less fearful. Her research team also found that those who valued self-transcendence—or thinking beyond oneself—wanted to feel more empathy and compassion for others. On the other hand, those that valued "self-enhancement" (personal power) wanted to feel more anger and pride.

How might this play out in school? Perhaps a student who values openness to change will jump into new creative projects or activities, while one who appreciates conservation may be more comfortable with traditional approaches to subject matter (lectures, worksheets). A colleague who values self-transcendence may be skilled at empathic, active listening, while one raised to value self-enhancement may advocate for their opinions more frequently and assertively.

Jeanne Tsai's research suggests that American and some East Asian cultures differ in their preference for high-arousal positive affective states (excitement, enthusiasm) and low-arousal positive affective states (calm, peacefulness) (Tsai et al. 2006). Many American teachers feel more motivated when their students appear happy and excited during a class discussion, while some East Asian teachers prefer to see calm and reflective responses during group interactions.

With this in mind, consider how your own upbringing has influenced your beliefs about appropriate emotional expression. As you unpack your beliefs, you may see how they influence your (often implicit) judgments of others.

An Action

This week, take the opportunity to explore your beliefs about your emotions more deeply. To what degree do you currently agree or disagree with the following statements (adapted from Ford and Gross 2019)? Rate your level of agreement (1–10).

- Emotions are basically bad.

- Emotions cannot be expressed in words.

- I cannot change the way I feel.

- Intense emotions are dangerous.

- It's not appropriate to express emotions with students.

- It's not appropriate to express emotions with colleagues.

- High-intensity emotions are uncontrollable.

Guiding Questions

What are your strongest, most powerful beliefs? If you could shift just one of these beliefs, which would it be? Why?

Take a few minutes to brainstorm the possible benefits of approaching this belief differently. For example, if you were taught that any form of emotional expression is "bad," what would happen if you started to believe differently? How might that shift affect your own well-being and your relationships with others? Map out the possibilities.

Changing your beliefs may feel like a tall order, and it can take time. So why do it? Because teachers who suppress emotions that they don't feel are appropriate may pay a cost in the form of emotional exhaustion (Donker et al. 2020). In fact, researchers have found that suppressing unpleasant emotions may be linked to greater anxiety, anger, and frustration (M. Lee et al. 2016).

Benefits

Untangling the beliefs that hurt us may be the key to greater emotional resilience. The good news here is that teachers benefit much more from shifting their interpretations than they do from suppressing what they feel. We feel less exhausted, anxious, and angry, and we enjoy our work more (Donker et al. 2020; M. Lee et al. 2016).

How do you change your beliefs? Begin by becoming aware of the inner voice that makes judgments (*You are weak because you feel sad right now.*), and start questioning them (*Why isn't it okay to feel sad?*). You can learn to be with those feelings because you've learned how legitimate they are. As we've said, emotions are information, and they can serve as tools to guide your decisions and behaviors.

Additional Resources

- "Teaching Your Heart Out: Emotional Labor and the Need for Systemic Change," *Edutopia,* https://www.edutopia.org/article/teaching-your-heart-out-emotional -labor-and-need-systemic-change

- Jeanne Tsai, "How Culture Influences Emotion," https://stanfordconnects.stanford .edu/watch/how-culture-influences-emotion/

Week 18: Challenging Your Thoughts and Beliefs

I just can't connect with this student. I don't have the energy for this anymore. I'm a bad teacher. Do any of these statements ring true for you? Typically, we say such things to ourselves after a stressful event. Perhaps we've hung up the phone after a charged conversation with a parent. Maybe a lesson or school day has been particularly rough. Or we're trying to do our best each day and struggling due to a lack of time, technology, training, or emotional stamina.

During times of distress, we may be flooded with anger, frustration, fear, or despair, so that some of the things we say to ourselves can *feel* true. Problem is—if the internal monologue continues (*I can't do this!*), the statements can become *beliefs* about ourselves.

A Pathway

If only you could approach that event—that conversation with a parent, the blank-faced stares from students during online teaching, or a public health crisis—with some level of detachment. Difficult things happen. So what happens when things don't go as hoped or planned?

Research tells us that our thoughts about the things that happen to us can have a powerful effect on our feelings and behaviors (Beck 1996). They trigger a whole cycle of responses, as in the following example:

1. Event: I receive negative feedback from a supervisor.

2. Thought: I tell myself something like, *I am never going to get this right.*

3. Emotion: I feel shame, frustration, anger, fear, disgust—or a combination.

4. Behavior: I do something: respond defensively, withdraw, and avoid the supervisor, or disengage from my work for a while.

You can interrupt the thought-feeling-behavior loop. One way is to regularly question your thinking in a structured way. *Cognitive reappraisal*—one of the most well-researched methods for navigating stressful experiences—shifts your interpretation of a situation. It can lessen both emotional and physical feelings of anxiety while reducing depression (Hofmann et al. 2012). If you practice cognitive reappraisal regularly, you can begin to adjust your perspective, minimize intense emotions, and ultimately respond more thoughtfully to students and colleagues.

For example, if a student yells at you in class, you might think, *This is awful; it feels terrible to be yelled at in front of all these kids. What did I do to deserve this?* However, when you pause and reassess the situation—in the moment or later in the day—you may find yourself beginning to adjust your thinking. For example, *What's the worst thing that could happen here? What am I imagining this means? Is my thought true or accurate? Can I look at this student's anger another way?* The result may be, *That wasn't pleasant, but it's likely that this student is having a really rough time right now. It wasn't personal.* With this different perspective, you're less likely to react angrily—and you're more likely to help your student find constructive outlets for their anger.

A shift in perspective doesn't happen without a little effort, but by asking yourself a few brief questions, you may find yourself interpreting the circumstances differently and feel your emotions lessen in intensity.

An Action

Choose a recent situation at work that was difficult for you emotionally and tapped irrational thoughts. In your journal, describe the situation. Then answer the following questions:

- What am I thinking, imagining, or telling myself about the situation?

- How do those thoughts make me feel?

- What makes me think the thought is true or accurate?

- What makes me think the thought is not true or, at least, not completely true?

- Is there another way to look at this? What is it?

- Is there an action I can take right now, now that I have more perspective?

Guiding Questions

Describe how your feelings or thoughts about this event shifted after you answered all the questions. Which questions were most useful to you? When might you draw on these questions again?

Benefits

Because cognitive reappraisal is a go-to strategy for reducing depression and anxiety (Llewellyn et al. 2013; Troy et al. 2010), researchers are studying its role in teachers' daily lives. A recent study tracked middle school teachers' cortisol levels throughout a school year. Cortisol, a chemical marker of stress, tended to rise in the spring and drop again in the fall. However, researchers found that cognitive reappraisal helped to buffer teachers' stress response throughout the year—and it was much more effective than suppressing emotions (Katz et al. 2018).

If you incorporate this strategy for navigating your emotions, it could be one of the most effective tools in your repertoire. Just like physical exercise, however, this isn't something to try once or twice—it's a practice.

As you begin to challenge your thinking on a regular basis, you'll experience a shift in the intensity of your feelings. Telling yourself, *I'm a bad teacher,* in the middle of a global crisis may even feel silly once you practically acknowledge the real challenges in your path. Simply extending kindness to yourself and lowering your expectations may help a lot, too. As teachers, we are doing our best with the resources in front of us, and every day is a victory when we show up with the best we have to offer.

Additional Resources

- "Challenging Your Thoughts and Beliefs," *Greater Good in Education,* https://ggie .berkeley.edu/practice/challenging-your-thoughts-and-beliefs

- Judith S. Beck, *Cognitive Behavior Therapy: Basics and Beyond*

- David Burns, *Feeling Great: The Revolutionary New Treatment for Depression and Anxiety*

Week 19: Being Kind to Yourself

Now that you are more aware of some of the things you say to yourself, you can practice being gentler with yourself.

Those of us drawn to education may be pretty good at extending kindness and compassion to our students, but what about ourselves? Mindfulness teacher Jack Kornfield reminds us, "If your compassion doesn't include yourself, it is incomplete." And at times, our own looming, menacing thoughts can work against us.

When we face potential physical threats, like a car speeding toward us, our fight-or-flight-or-freeze response kicks into gear, triggering a series of chemical responses to protect ourselves from harm. This is part of our "reptilian" brain, built into our biology early in our evolution—when the threat was a hungry predator, not a car.

However, when self-critical thoughts appear (*I can't keep up with these demands!* or *I'm a failure as a teacher!*), we *also* experience a palpable threat—to our self-concept. Our bodies don't know the difference—this threat sparks a similar stress response in our reptilian brain. And in this case, self-criticism is particularly problematic—we are both the attacker and the attacked.

Compassion scholar Paul Gilbert (2009) explains that our threatened nervous systems benefit when we draw on our mammalian "affiliative" and self-soothing system. As we learn to engage our mammalian soothing system to calm our reptilian threat system, we begin to reduce the effects of shame, worry, and rumination—*natural* human responses to threatening thoughts and beliefs.

A Pathway

Self-compassion can be a salve when we face our own menacing thoughts. Researcher Kristin Neff (2011) describes self-compassion as "the practice of quieting the inner critic, replacing it with a voice of support, understanding, and care for oneself." In other words, when you practice self-compassion, you treat yourself as you would treat a close friend who is struggling.

Let's say your friend just realized that they taught a math lesson incorrectly. They feel foolish, embarrassed, ashamed. What would you say? What would you do? I would approach them quietly and calmly and say something like, "Hey, I can see that you feel bad right now. It's okay. You're okay. You know, I have several friends who have done this. And I make mistakes all the time. We all do. You're an amazing, committed teacher.

I hope you can cut yourself some slack and be kind to yourself." Then I would probably reassure them with a gentle squeeze of their arm or shoulder, or offer a hug. How might it feel to treat yourself in this way?

Self-compassion, as a practice, taps into the mammalian caregiving system, cuing us to draw on things like warmth, gentle vocalizations, and soothing touch. We are physically wired to be comforted by these things. It may be difficult to imagine responding to your own calming touch or quiet voice, but consider how people respond to a raised voice versus a gentle one—and why it's common to say, "Give yourself a pat on the back." Many of us didn't have caregivers who reassured us or gathered us in their arms when we were hurt, yet we humans are wired for touch and connection (Linden 2015).

Researchers Kristin Neff and Chris Germer (2013) identify three components to a self-compassionate response when you are experiencing emotional pain: mindfulness, common humanity, and self-kindness. First, you openly acknowledge your own suffering, taking a nonjudgmental stance toward your perceived inadequacies (without suppressing or exaggerating your feelings); next, you remember that others experience this form of suffering and that you aren't alone in this experience; finally, you extend kindness toward yourself.

Imagine you're experiencing a particularly rough day. You're teaching an online class, and the students are more and more disengaged each day. It's discouraging. In fact, it feels like it's rare for your students to even respond aloud to your questions these days.

In this case, you take a few minutes to pause between classes to identify what you're feeling and offer yourself some reassurance.

- Mindfulness—acknowledge suffering: *Wow, it's tough to sense my students' disengagement right now. I feel helpless in this moment.*

- Common humanity—you're not alone: *No doubt other teachers feel this frustration, too. Online teaching isn't always conducive to sustained student engagement— face-to-face teaching isn't always either!*

- Self-kindness—extend kindness to yourself: *This is a tough time right now, so I'm going to give myself a little hug of encouragement. I'm a committed teacher. I'm doing my best—and it's going to be okay. One day at a time.*

Does this sound a little too sweet and touchy-feely? Many of us think we need to beat ourselves up to motivate ourselves. In fact, some critics argue that self-compassion is potentially weak, self-indulgent, or even selfish. However, self-compassion research findings demonstrate the opposite. People who score highly on self-compassion scales are more motivated and physically healthy, are less susceptible to burnout, and are more likely to reach out to others (Breines and Chen 2012; Dunne et al. 2018; Neff and Pommier 2013; Terry and Leary 2011), because people with a high level of self-compassion experience less fear of failure and a greater sense of personal responsibility.

If this seems counterintuitive, consider what it feels like to be shamed for not meeting an expectation (e.g., when a parent reprimands a child for failing a Spanish test). How motivating is that? If that parent approached the child by acknowledging the failed test ("Wow, that doesn't feel good. I'm sorry."), reassuring the child that they aren't alone in this experience ("I really struggled in Spanish, too."), and offered support ("How can I help? What do you need right now?"), then the child would be more likely to respond with hope—and a plan for next steps.

Of course, a few moments of self-compassion will not suddenly shift your perspective about yourself, but with time and practice, self-compassion is a skill that can be learned. And here are some further benefits: it can bolster life satisfaction, happiness, self-confidence, and well-being (Zessin et al. 2015) while reducing anxiety, depression, stress, perfectionism, shame, body dissatisfaction, and disordered eating (T. D. Braun et al. 2016). More self-compassionate individuals who work in service professions like counseling also report lower fatigue and burnout compared to their less self-compassionate counterparts (Beaumont et al. 2016).

An Action

Now that you know how to practice self-compassion and how it might benefit you, it's time to try it. When you face a challenging event or thought this week at home or at school, tell yourself this: *This thing I'm dealing with is tough.* Then, acknowledge that you're not alone in facing this issue. Other people face it, too. Finally, offer yourself some kind or compassionate words, a pat on the back, or a reassuring squeeze. Commit to trying this practice several times this week and consider how it affects your mind and body.

Guiding Questions

What did you appreciate about this practice? How did you speak to yourself? Did a change in tone or a gentle touch feel reassuring and soothing—or awkward? Why or why not?

Did you notice any difference in your nervous system before and after this practice—a shift in breathing, heart rate, muscle tension? How did you respond to each of the three elements of self-compassion: mindfulness; common humanity—realizing you are not alone; and self-kindness? When was it most helpful to engage in this brief practice? Why?

Benefits

We live in a world overrun with expectations and judgments. It's no wonder many of us get caught up in internalizing those expectations. When we carry around a performance orientation, we can spend a lot of time navigating potential threats to our sense of "success."

No one wants to feel fundamentally faulty, isolated, or unacceptable. Self-compassion research changes the conversation entirely. When we're self-compassionate, we accept the fact that there will be pain to navigate and that mistakes will be made. And that's okay. Regardless of the outcome—that missed deadline or that incomprehensible lesson—we pat ourselves on the back and keep going.

What might happen if you fully embraced the value of *being* who you are rather than *doing* or performing? What if you learned to befriend your flawed, real, beautiful self?

Additional Resources

- Kristin Neff, *Self-Compassion: The Proven Power of Being Kind to Yourself*

- "Self-Compassion for Adults," *Greater Good in Education,* https://ggie.berkeley .edu/my-well-being/self-compassion-for-adults/#tab__

Week 20: Creating a Resilience Plan

Last week as I was leading a webinar about the importance of self-care and emotional resilience, a district leader in the group somewhat jokingly threw a comment into the online chat box: "I don't need another thing on my to-do list. Just the mention of to-do lists stresses me out." No doubt, you might relate. I do. However, you likely picked up this book because you want to experience greater well-being, and you realize that taking care of yourself is essential. In fact, scholars argue that self-care is an ethical imperative. "Self-care is not a luxury. It is a human requisite, a professional necessity, and an ethical imperative" (Norcross and Guy 2007). Why?

A Pathway

The primary way children learn social-emotional skills is through exposure to adult behavior and modeling. They regulate their nervous systems with ours. In fact, recent studies link teacher burnout with student stress. When researchers in British Columbia collected saliva samples from over 400 elementary school children in 17 schools and tested their cortisol levels, they found that in classrooms where teachers experienced more burnout or feelings of emotional exhaustion, students' cortisol levels were higher (Oberle and Schonert-Reichl 2016). In addition, in a pilot study of 171 kindergarteners and 33 teachers, researchers linked teacher stress with children's executive functions (mental processes that help us to plan, remember, think flexibly, and control our impulses). In only low-poverty schools (as opposed to high-poverty schools), students experienced fewer gains in executive functions when teachers experienced high stress (Neuenschwander et al. 2017).

Stress may be contagious, but peace is contagious, too. When teachers participate in programs that feature emotion-regulation strategies and mindfulness practices, they report improvements in personal well-being *and* their ability to provide emotional support in their classrooms (Jennings 2015). They're also more efficient in their use of instructional time, and their students reported higher engagement and motivation. So, prioritizing your own well-being can also lead to more effective teaching and engagement with students and colleagues. You deserve it—and your students will reap the benefits, too.

At this point in your journey through this book, you've explored ways to understand and navigate your emotions (month 1), learned how to be more mindfully aware of your experiences (month 2), and discovered strategies for recognizing and savoring positive experiences (months 3 and 4). And this month, you've examined some of your beliefs about emotions and emotional expression, practiced questioning your thoughts and beliefs, and offered yourself kindness and self-compassion during some of your more challenging moments. Of course, evidence-based strategies for emotional resilience also include things like regular physical exercise, social connection, good nutrition, and a reliable sleep schedule (Ozbay et al. 2007; Penedo and Dahn 2005).

Yet all these activities require practice and repetition. It's one thing to know about them; it's another to commit to taking regular action. So it's time to check in with yourself to determine the next steps. If your emotional resilience and wellness are priorities for you, you may already have a set of habits that support your goals (Galla and Duckworth 2015)—a nutrition plan or a weekly social connection with a friend. Perhaps now is a good time to tweak those and recalibrate? Is there something else you might want to prioritize?

And if you haven't established daily habits yet, no problem. Here is an opportunity. Self-care doesn't need to be another "should" for your to-do list. It's something you can easily weave into your day. Keep it simple.

An Action

As you consider the weekly "actions" you've taken over the past several months, are there any strategies or practices you want to welcome into your daily life? These activities can become part of an easy, straightforward, personal resilience plan. Try the following:

1. Choose one or two self-care practices to implement each day (or almost every day) for at least five minutes at a time. (What appeals most to you at this time in your school year?)

2. Describe the practice (a savoring strategy, a mindfulness practice, a self-compassion break). What will you do?

3. Decide when and where you will practice this strategy (e.g., listen to a five-minute body scan each night on your phone, or practice identifying and challenging one or two unpleasant thoughts every morning in your journal). It's important to be concrete and specific here, but one sentence is fine.

Guiding Questions

It's not too difficult to choose a new habit, right? The challenge is facing the stressors and obstacles that may prevent you from implementing the habit. People who are successful in changing their habits can anticipate problems and plan for how to navigate them (Orbell and Sheeran 2000). Ask yourself the following before you begin:

- What kinds of obstacles do I anticipate (e.g., forgetting, feeling too stressed, impatience, self-criticism)?

- What are some of the ways that I can evade those obstacles?

- Who can help keep me accountable for this simple plan?

Then, at the end of the week, revisit these questions. What obstacles did you face? How will you move forward from here?

To help you on your way, here are a few research-based tips for creating long-term habits:

- Change your environment by removing distractions (find a quiet place for mindfulness practice or set boundaries around morning and evening communication).

- Provide yourself with physical reminders and cues to support your habits (set a notification or alarm on your phone or put a sticky note on your computer) (Norcross et al. 2002).

- Rely on a social network or a friend to encourage and motivate you (exercise with friends, share daily "awe" experiences with a colleague, or record three good things each day with your students on your class bulletin board) (Kramer et al. 2014).

- Offer yourself encouraging messages and positive affirmations along the way (repeat a favorite quote or tell yourself what you would tell a friend after they wrote in their gratitude journal three days in a row—or didn't). We can frame messages to ourselves that motivate action by emphasizing the benefits of the habit we're targeting (*Another day of healthy eating means that I feel lighter and more energetic!*) (Gerend and Maner 2011).

Benefits

You're important. Your work is important. And your well-being matters. As you take these simple steps each day, you will likely notice your mood shifting (Mazzucchelli et al. 2010). And your efforts will benefit not only you but also those around you.

You and your colleagues' daily acts of self-care may be transformational in the long run—acts on behalf of larger systems change. According to a report by the Robert Wood Johnson Foundation, one of the top six barriers to educational equity is actually "educator stress and burnout" (Simmons et al. 2018).

Perhaps not surprisingly then, Elena Aguilar, author of *Onward* and *Coaching for Equity* says, "In order to create the just and equitable society that I know so many of us yearn for, we need tremendous reserves of resilience." If we want to transform the way we do education, we need to start here, with ourselves—welcoming a culture of self-care.

Additional Resources

- "To Change Yourself, Change Your World," *Greater Good,* https://greatergood
.berkeley.edu/article/item/to_change_yourself_change_your_world

- "My Well-Being," *Greater Good in Education,* https://ggie.berkeley.edu/my-well
-being/self-compassion-for-adults/#tab__3

Honoring Your Strengths

Something was beating in my soul
a fever or lost wings
and I made my own way
deciphering
that fire.

—Pablo Neruda, "La Poesía"

My daughter recently started working in a teen mental health program. Her work is emotionally grueling, but yesterday she texted me a photo of a handwritten note she received from a soon-to-be graduate: "Oh my goodness. Where do I start? You helped me feel confident in my skills and you always gave me a sense of serenity amidst the chaos. I aspire to be like you, and I really respect you for being such an independent person. Thank you for caring about me throughout my good and bad days. Also, sorry about fainting.—♥"

This will be the first of many notes, no doubt. I have a drawer of them myself, and I dive into those precious thank-you cards, photos, and drawings on days when I lose touch with my *why.* Of course, we don't always receive the external validation we desire from our students or colleagues, which is why it's so important to regularly revisit, clarify, and honor what *we* bring to our work.

For the last several months, we've explored actions you can take to navigate stressors in your life and how to find and acknowledge goodness in the world. This month we will be unearthing the goodness in you by considering your values and character strengths, what is meaningful to you in your life and career, and how you might sharpen and clarify your purpose at work.

Week 21: Acknowledging Your Values

We ended last month with a focus on self-compassion—the willingness to treat your human, imperfect self as you would treat a good friend. A self-compassionate approach to life prompts us to *be* with and accept ourselves, regardless of what we accomplish in life. Rather than connecting your worth to *what* you do and *how well* you do it, your compassionate self accepts the "good" and the "bad" and honors the whole package of you—especially when you stumble.

Yet it can be difficult not to see our faults as threats to our own well-being. You may remember reading about the "negativity bias" a few weeks ago—we humans are wired to remember the bad things that happen to us, because our bodies automatically respond to potential threats to our physical and psychological safety (Hanson 2009). In other words, you may not remember the ten positive teacher evaluations you received, but you can't forget that one stinging comment from the student who didn't like your teaching style.

This month, we're taking a different approach. Rather than focusing on stressors, threats, and challenges—which undoubtedly exist—we're considering your strengths. But this exploration isn't about your skill set or your talents. Forget the performance orientation for now.

A Pathway

A few decades ago, a psychologist named Martin Seligman introduced a new approach to psychology that shifted the conversation. Rather than focusing on the conditions like anxiety and depression, he proposed an entirely different orientation to human behavior—one focused on strengths. The ideas he shared back in 1998, when he was president of the American Psychological Association, grew into what is called the "positive psychology movement," which aspires to make our lives more fulfilling and meaningful—as an alternative to simply managing mental health conditions. Since then, many psychologists and social workers have jumped on the bandwagon to focus on our potential for flourishing, which includes positive emotions, engagement, relationships, meaning, and accomplishments (see Additional Resources).

The core assumption of this strengths-based lens is that all human beings have assets and abilities that we can draw on for greater well-being (Saleeby 2008). As an educational professional, you may already be aware of the positive psychology movement. If not, you may be a proponent of a strengths-based focus—especially when you think about student learning and personal growth. However, it's worth considering how you apply this perspective to your own personal and professional development.

Rather than focusing on problem solving or "problems of practice" in our teaching and policy making, it's worth identifying and leveraging our strengths. However, we're going to broaden the discussion to address the values and personal qualities that drive us in our work. In other words, your content knowledge and technical expertise fall into a different category for a different conversation. Right now, it's important to consider the principles (or virtues) that undergird your relationships both at work and at home. For example, researchers who interviewed teachers about their personal strengths discovered that those strengths fall into three categories of larger virtues—including performance virtues like resilience, relational virtues like empathy, and emotional virtues like enthusiasm and love (Arthur et al. 2015). And when asked to comment on the ideal strengths of a teacher, the top six included fairness, love of learning, creativity, humor, perseverance, and leadership.

One study of six hundred teachers in Turkey suggests that qualities like academic optimism, hope, and zest for work can predict teachers' self-efficacy and sense of success (Sezgin and Erdogan 2015); and in another study of several hundred Italian teachers, researchers connected teachers' values with their sense of self-efficacy, which also predicted positive student learning outcomes (Barni et al. 2019). This magical element of "self-efficacy," the belief that you can do your job well, can be a real driving force in maintaining motivation at work. Linking these factors together—values, strengths, self-efficacy, and motivation—researchers argue that a strengths-based focus for pre-service teachers can help them to clarify their beliefs and values while also bolstering their motivation and teaching efficacy early in their careers (He 2009). What are the values that drive you in your work? How do they play out in your day-to-day interactions?

Chris Peterson and Martin Seligman (2004) developed a strengths framework captured in a widely used assessment tool called the Values in Action (VIA) Inventory of Strengths. This classification system—which serves as a counterpoint to the diagnostic and statistical manual of mental disorders used to identify human deficits—features twenty-four universally valued character strengths that fall under six overarching virtues. Research links these twenty-four strengths to well-being outcomes like life satisfaction, confidence, and a sense of purpose (Niemiec 2013). You can take this free assessment yourself.

An Action

Carve out fifteen to twenty minutes to take the free VIA survey that will identify the character strengths that are most important to you. (See Additional Resources for the link.)

Then, reflect on the results by answering the following questions. (It's one thing to take a quick survey; it's another to dig in and consider why these character strengths rose to the surface for you. I encourage you to take the time to answer these questions as thoughtfully as possible.)

Guiding Questions

1. According to the VIA survey, what are your top five values in action (or character strengths)?

2. List each strength and describe why it is important to you.

3. Describe one or two ways you currently demonstrate this value in action—both at home and at work.

4. How does it feel to reflect on these values in action? In what ways do they feed, motivate, or energize you?

5. Finally, identify one value in action that is a priority for you but wasn't captured by the survey as one of your "top five." Why is it important? How have you enacted this value at home and at work? Finally, in what ways might you prioritize this value in action? List several examples.

Benefits

By now, you may be sensing the importance of tuning in to your values because they help to clarify your sense of meaning as an educator. When you shift your thinking away from teaching as a technical skill driven by standards and evaluated by performances and toward the notion of educating—which is undergirded by values, character strengths, and dynamic, enlivening relationships—your work takes on an entirely different energy and momentum.

Your character strengths not only serve as guides for you but also motivate and inspire your students. When researchers asked college students to reflect on their teachers' characters and how they affected them positively, the most frequently identified character strengths were "wisdom and knowledge," "humanity," and "transcendence"—that ability to think beyond your own self-interest and act with empathy and compassion for others (Majid et al. 2014).

Of course, the universal character strengths you value don't have to align perfectly with your students or colleagues. However, they need to feel right and authentic to you. One of my favorite quotes comes from educational philosopher and activist Parker Palmer, who simply states, "We teach who we are."

Lifting up and enacting your values with a personal sense of integrity can charge you up with a greater sense of meaning and purpose in your work. And when you engage with others with a clear sense of your own identity, they will feel it, too.

Additional Resources

- "The VIA Character Strengths Survey," https://www.viacharacter.org/survey/account/register

- Martin Seligman, *Flourish: A Visionary New Understanding of Happiness and Well-Being*

- Parker Palmer, *The Courage to Teach*

Week 22: Affirming Your Character Strengths

On our walk this morning, my husband told me all about Mrs. Carter. After his parents' divorce, he moved into a new community as a sixth grader. At home, his alcoholic mom was checked out much of the time, but at school, there was Mrs. Carter. She had a sparkle in her brown eyes and a curiosity that excited him as she shared her love of learning with the class. And that curiosity translated to him, too. "She was the first person who really saw me," says my husband. And that was also the first time he felt energized at school—reflected in his straight As. You may also have a Mrs. Carter in your past. Perhaps there was a teacher who ignited your own "spark."

You have identified and reflected on some of the values that inform your passion for education—in the form of "character strengths." At this point, it's worth considering how they come alive in your relationships at school and at home.

A Pathway

Let's take this exploration a step further as you examine what it means to show up in the world with your strengths. According to the VIA Institute on Character, "Character Strengths are the positive parts of your personality that impact how you think, feel, and behave" (https://viacharacter.org/character-strengths-via). After taking the survey last week, you may have determined that your top five strengths are hope, humility, honesty, kindness, and perseverance. And after reflecting on them, you have a better idea of why they motivate you. For example, you can't imagine teaching without a sense of hope in your students or in the school systems and policies you are striving to change on behalf of those students. Or maybe what you know, for sure, is that honesty is the foundation of all your relationships because it is wrapped up in your desire to form safe and trusting connections with your students or colleagues.

Positive psychology tends to focus on having and using your strengths, and several studies provide some clues about what it looks and feels like to draw on your strengths at work. Alex M. Wood and his colleagues (2011) developed a Strengths Use Scale and tested it to see whether tapping into your strengths leads to greater well-being. After surveying over two hundred participants three times across six months, they found that strengths use seemed to lead to less stress and more positive emotions, self-esteem, and vitality.

Another study's findings suggest that people who intentionally apply their strengths on the job have more positive experiences, including greater job satisfaction, pleasure, engagement, and meaning—as well as a strong sense of a "calling" in their work (Harzer and Ruch 2012). Interestingly, study participants reported greater benefits when they applied four to seven strengths rather than three or fewer. In fact, out of the twenty-four strengths in the VIA survey, most of us do have three to seven "signature" strengths that we tend to enjoy practicing (Peterson and Seligman 2004).

When you think about how to apply character strengths to your teaching, the discussion gets richer and even more interesting. For example, a couple of faculty members at Arizona State University used the VIA survey as a reflective tool to inform educators' personal and professional development (McGovern and Miller 2008). They proposed innovative ways for educators to link their twenty-eight signature strengths from the VIA survey with a "checklist" of twenty-eight teacher qualities and corresponding behaviors (Keeley et al. 2006) so that they could explore how their strengths or qualities might play out more meaningfully in the classroom.

For example, if being humble emerged as a quality you value, you might readily admit your mistakes—a great way to inspire both risk-taking and psychological safety in the classroom. If creativity is a strength you privilege, you may be more likely to try out innovative teaching methods or pepper your explanations with highly relevant, personal examples as you teach. The idea here is to draw on assessment tools like these to stimulate reflection about how your strengths and values invigorate your teaching.

An Action

However, one of the most effective positive psychology interventions you can draw on to tap your strengths is quite simple (Seligman et al. 2005). This week, choose one personal strength that you value, like courage, teamwork, or humor. (You may choose one of your "signature" strengths from your VIA survey result—or one you'd like to emulate more frequently.) Next, consider a simple way you might use this strength each day for a week, and then act on your idea whenever the opportunity arises. For example, if you want to capitalize on kindness as a strength, you might perform a random act of kindness for a colleague, write a note of appreciation to a student, or volunteer at a food bank in your community over the weekend.

Guiding Questions

At the end of the week, reflect on the following questions in your journal:

- What strength did you choose? Why?

- What activities or actions did you choose to act on that strength?

- How did it feel to enact your strength each day?

- What did you learn about yourself after a week of consciously sharing this strength or quality with others?

Benefits

Tapping your strengths in this way can increase well-being and reduce symptoms of depression (Seligman et al. 2005). Of course, this is a concrete, activity-based approach to living your values, which might be criticized as somewhat mechanistic (Banicki 2014).

However, the big-picture idea here is to draw on your values and strengths to inform the way you show up in the world. In this sense, the positive psychology movement's focus on character strengths can help us to be more aware of the way we like to "be" at work and at home, which is also a great model for our students. When researcher Shawn Ginwright (2018) proposed a model for "healing-centered" schools and classrooms, he prompted educators to shift their internal questioning of students from "What is wrong with you?" or even "What happened to you?" to "What is *right* with you?" It's easy for us all to focus on our weaknesses and personal challenges, but when we spend time making the most of our positive qualities, we can build greater self-esteem, confidence, and a sense of connectedness to others.

Additional Resources

- "Teacher Behavior Checklist," https://www.usf.edu/atle/documents/handout-qualilties-effective-teacher-tbc.pdf

- "Use Your Strengths," *Greater Good in Education,* https://ggie.berkeley.edu/practice/use-your-strengths/#tab__2

Week 23: Recognizing Your Meaningful Work

Many teachers are experiencing burnout—exhaustion, cynicism, and a sense of ineffi-cacy in their work. Even if you feel committed to your work, it can be difficult to see your way through the haze of stressors at times. So perhaps it's helpful to check in with yourself right now and ask, "What gives me a sense of meaning in my work, even on the tough days?"

I asked some of my friends and colleagues this question, and here are a few of their responses. "When my students make me laugh, and when they do that 'oooh' sound that kids do when they finally get it," confessed a fifth-grade teacher. "Knowing the work you do is bigger than yourself is what keeps me motivated," said a university professor. A twenty-year kindergarten teacher said this: "It's still the relationships I build every year that give me the most meaning."

Of course, educators tend to have noble and selfless ideals. We want to work on behalf of students who are vulnerable and benefit from our care and advocacy. Yet our own drive to do meaningful work can work against us as we experience vicarious or secondary stress and potential burnout. Teachers, in a recent study conducted by Tom Brunzell and his colleagues (2018), share some of the fundamental challenges of their work. One says, "You think it's about teaching them academics, and then you meet your students and their many social skills and well-being needs." While another teacher admits, "Emotionally, you don't ever leave the job."

A Pathway

Brunzell and his team (2018) found that teachers working with students affected by significant trauma identified two primary sources of "meaningful work" that helped them to navigate some of the more enduring stressors identified above. First, teachers identified their work as "meaningful" when they had effective instructional strategies to engage their students and support positive behavior. Second, teachers found their work to be meaningful when they experienced greater well-being, including coping strategies that worked for them, a positive sense of their identity as a teacher, and strong relation-ships with colleagues. When teachers acknowledged the challenges to their work and developed sources of support like teaching tools and well-being practices, they were also more likely to pursue four additional pathways of meaning.

These four pathways are individuation, contribution, self-connection, and unification (Rosso et al. 2010). First, when you experience individuation, your meaningful actions help to flesh out your sense of self as someone who does valuable and worthy work. In other words, what you do defines who you are. Second, contribution means that your meaningful actions serve something bigger or greater than you. You believe that your work has a larger impact on the world. Third, self-connection reflects your integrity. Your meaningful actions grow to align with the way you see yourself. Finally, unification signifies that your meaningful actions bring you "into harmony" with others and your own principles. For example, your work may also enhance your relationships with students and colleagues, and their relationships with each other. And you may feel more whole as you act out your own values and character strengths in the process.

Researchers find that some of the primary sources of meaningful work come from ourselves, and others from the work itself or our own spiritual life (Rosso et al. 2010). Perhaps you won't be surprised to read that the study of "meaningful work" emerged out of positive psychology research, and a sense of "meaning" is one of the key conditions for "flourishing" individuals and communities (Seligman and Csikszentmihalyi 2000).

Of course, there are many other benefits to meaningful work. It correlates with greater job commitment satisfaction and engagement, a larger sense of life satisfaction and meaning, as well as greater physical health (B. A. Allen et al. 2019). In other studies with educators, meaningful work appears to serve as a resource that can mitigate the harm of work stressors while enhancing teachers' perceived well-being, physical health, and resilience (Minkkinen et al. 2020; Van Wingerden and Poell 2019). So even if you work in a stressful classroom or school, your sense of meaning can serve as a protective factor.

An Action

At this point, it is helpful to explore why you were drawn to this career in the first place. When you look back at your life, can you identify three to five key moments that may have influenced your decision to work in the field of education? You may have discovered something about yourself, internally, or you may have experienced an event or circumstance that clarified your values. Map out these moments on paper with images or symbols and describe them briefly.

Guiding Questions

After you identify these key touchpoints in your life, reflect on each moment and consider how it relates to the meaningful work you do now. Here are some questions for journaling:

- Which of the following influenced your decision to pursue a career in education—yourself, others, a work experience or life circumstance, or something else?

- Reflect on how or why these influences were significant to you then.

- As you have continued in your work, which of the four pathways (individuation, contribution, self-connection, unification) enliven and invigorate your sense of meaning? Why?

- What does work in your classroom, school, or larger community mean to you right now?

Benefits

After reflecting on what brought you to this profession and the sources of meaningful work in your life, you may not be surprised to know that recognizing and nurturing your own sense of meaning can enhance your ability to care for your students. One study of thirty-three teachers linked students' reports that their teachers cared for them with teachers' reported sense of meaning. Further, students' perceptions of teacher care, as they played out in the teacher-student relationship, also appeared to influence students' self-esteem, well-being, and school engagement (Lavy and Naama-Ghanayim 2020).

Researcher Michael Steger (2019) reminds us that meaningful work can be a "renewable resource," but not when we're expending all our energy day after day. We must be able to invest in ourselves in the first place, strive for "work-life harmony," and be honest with ourselves about how our work can take a toll on our well-being, which ultimately necessitates collective action as well. (See Additional Resources.)

To do meaningful work, we need a variety of supports, including work tasks, conditions, and collegial relationships that enhance our ability to teach and reach our students—as well as professional development opportunities that invigorate our sense of meaning as educational professionals (Janik and Rothmann 2015). We can celebrate and elevate the ways that our work enlivens us while advocating for the supports we need to continue making meaningful work a "renewable resource."

Additional Resources

- Brian Dik, Zinta Byrne, and Michael Steger (eds.), *Purpose and Meaning in the Workplace*

- "Does a Meaningful Job Need to Burn You Out?," *Greater Good,* https://greatergood.berkeley.edu/article/item/does_a_meaningful_job_need_to_burn_you_out

- "The Meaning in Life Questionnaire," http://www.michaelfsteger.com/?page_id=13

Week 24: Clarifying Your Purpose

When I was sixteen years old, Ms. Flora Kellogg invited me to teach her English literature classes on Student-Teacher day. The text that day was Coleridge's "Rime of the Ancient Mariner"—not a personal favorite of mine. Yet I vividly remember leaning back in her desk chair at the end of that day and feeling a strange combination of utter exhaustion, vitality, and joy. I was so tired that I cried, but that moment moved me closer to my purpose. Sure, I loved literature and the arts, but I realized that I thrived in contexts where I could facilitate discussions around the stuff of life. What does it mean to be human and alive in this world? How can we strive for mutual understanding *together?* Many other touchpoints inform my purpose, and you've already identified at least three key moments in your own life that brought you to this work.

There is a positive relationship between "meaningful work" and a sense of calling or purpose. The sense of meaning we experience at work can be enlivened and invigorated by our own purposeful actions, directing us toward what is "valuable"—either to our self, others, or both (Rosso et al. 2010; Willemse and Deacon 2015).

A Pathway

So what is "purpose," really? Psychologists claim that purpose is an intention to achieve a long-term goal that is personally meaningful and contributes something to the world (Damon et al. 2003). When we pursue a sense of purpose, these four things may be in play: dedicated commitment, personal meaningfulness, goal directedness, and a vision larger than oneself (Bronk et al. 2019).

You're likely aware of the importance of goals, in particular (and even encourage your students to set regular goals). Interestingly, people with purpose strive to meet a particular kind of goal. When Stanford researchers asked 1,200 American adults about their goals, they found that people with a greater sense of well-being pursued "beyond-the-self" goals, compared to people pursuing other types of goals. In other words, if your goal focuses on how you can help others (like your students), you may feel better than people with other types of goals (Bundick et al. 2021).

Studies link a strong sense of purpose to lower stress levels, increased physical health, higher cognitive functioning, and greater longevity (Fogelman and Canli 2015; Hill and Turiano 2014; Lewis et al. 2017). If you have some greater purpose that drives you—something to live for—you may be more likely to care for yourself on behalf of the cause.

Yet one study of teacher purpose tells us that educators don't necessarily define "purpose" in the same way researchers do—with reference to "personal meaning" and a "beyond-the-self" dimension (B. P. Quinn 2016). However, when asked more indirectly, Stanford researchers like Heather Malin (2018) seem to "get at" what matters to people with just a few simple questions (see the *Action* questions below).

With clear benefits to knowing the "why" behind your life and work, research suggests that people find purpose in their work by re-envisioning *how* their job aligns with their strengths, priorities, and passions. Amy Wrzesniewski and her team (2013) call this process "job crafting." Can you reconsider your job tasks and relationships—and the perceptions you have of both—so that you feel more engaged and fulfilled at work?

If we actively reconnect with our "why" (and how) on a regular basis, we're likely to experience greater well-being and motivation in our work and life—and our students reap the benefits. Knowing and sharing our sense of purpose with our colleagues and students can ultimately spark the same personal passions and get-up-and-go determination in those around us.

An Action

The following questions, developed by Stanford researchers, help teachers begin to clarify their sense of purpose (Malin 2018). Take a few minutes to write down your response to each question.

Personal Life:

- What are the three things that matter most to you?

- Why do they matter to you?

- When did they become important to you, and for how long will they be important?

- How do these things motivate and energize you?

Professional Life:

- Repeat the four questions above.

Goals and Activities:

- What specific goals or activities relate to your responses above?

- What are your most prominent goals right now?

- What activities do you spend the most time and energy on?

Guiding Questions

How do the things that matter most to you align with your professional goals and activities? Identify one or two simple changes you can make to your schedule so that you feel more energized and inspired in your work.

Benefits

In a recent study, high school teachers identified two primary things that gave them a sense of purpose at school: 1) their content area and 2) their relationships with students (B. P. Quinn 2016). More than content, the teachers I have informally surveyed tend to focus on the joy of witnessing student understanding and success, the sense of participating in something larger than themselves, and the deep satisfaction they gain from relationship building. We know that a sense of meaning and a drive toward purpose feed into teachers' positive attitudes about their work (Willemse and Deacon 2015). We can all benefit from support in enhancing our meaningful work—along with opportunities to share and celebrate common goals while developing a more purposeful vision together.

Additional Resources

- "How to Find Your Purpose in Life," *Greater Good,* https://greatergood.berkeley .edu/article/item/how_to_find_your_purpose_in_life

- Heather Malin, *Teaching for Purpose: Preparing Students for Lives of Meaning*

Celebrating Creativity

To practice any art, no matter how well or badly, is a way to make your soul grow. So do it.

—Kurt Vonnegut

When I find myself caught up in the more mundane, soul-sucking details of work, I tend to gravitate toward the arts. I'm an educator, but I'm also…a wannabe artist, and I admire humans who live life with a creative flourish. Academics may be my comfort zone, but art, literature, music, film, theatre—these expressions of life force—feed me and sustain me. It's a beautiful, spiritual thing to be carried along by a story, a photograph, a painting, or a moment of creativity. It can bring me back to myself and reconnect me with the world.

Month
7

I recently interviewed long-time educator Elena Aguilar, the author of *Onward: Cultivating Emotional Resilience for Educators,* and we talked about creativity as an energizing, resilience-building strategy. "There are a lot of things that human beings do that are concerning," she said, "but then, human beings create the most beautiful cave paintings; they sculpt things; they create beautiful temples, fabrics, jewelry, and meals. Creativity gives me hope for human beings. We love beauty just for the sake of beauty." Because the arts remind her of the beauty in humanity, she's exploring new ways to create by developing new soup recipes, writing, drawing, and making postcards.

You may not be a professional artist, but there may be moments in your life when you find yourself caught up in an activity you enjoy. Perhaps it's writing, knitting, gardening, dancing, or woodworking. Even reorganizing a closet, your garage, or your kitchen pantry can be gratifying. Whether we're bringing order to the chaos (inside or outside), seeing things with new eyes, solving problems, building something new, or redesigning a space, creativity may be an antidote to our "stuckness"—that sense of spiritual inertia that can weigh us down. Art and creativity can bring us back to ourselves, and this month we will rediscover creativity and the arts as vital forces in our lives.

Week 25: Appreciating "Third Things"

In graduate school, I savored the intellectual stimulation of my doctoral work and made new friends, yet many aspects of institutional life left me discouraged. The political infighting, arrogance, and superficial posturing gnawed away at me to the point that I'd sometimes ask myself, *Who am I in all of this? What's it all for?*

Then I came to one of the best decisions I've made. I signed up for a series of retreats for educational leaders. Each day the facilitators created simple, welcoming formats for reflection where we were each invited to explore how our work aligned with our larger sense of purpose in the world.

It's not always easy revealing your vulnerabilities, yearnings, and questions. For me, it feels like sacred work, and it requires trust. When we do share with one another on a deeper level, it can be incredibly rewarding.

A Pathway

"Third things" provide an access point for deeper sharing and meaning making. The retreat facilitators from the Center for Courage and Renewal used third things like poems, stories from different wisdom traditions, case studies, or works of art to spark reflection—where a few words from Mary Oliver or May Sarton expressed something I hadn't yet articulated for myself, or a single image I discovered in a line of photographs captured a facet of my emotional experience as a teacher.

Educational philosopher and activist Parker Palmer (2003) explains that third things "embody, or carry, the issue we want to focus on—and they allow the shy soul to speak about that issue without being scared off by the headlong, and headstrong, 'running at topics' so characteristic of academic discourse" (393). We use third things as tools that make us feel psychologically safe enough to "tell the truth, but tell it slant," as Emily Dickinson advised.

When you sit in a circle with a group of like-minded educators you've never met before and find yourself tiptoeing toward self-disclosure, you can feel quite vulnerable. Yet, when we dig in and share our fears and dreams with one another, the rewards can be great.

Back then, I didn't know a lot about the research connecting the arts with well-being. In fact, it's worth noting that forty-eight thousand people across thirty-three counties who engaged in arts-based activities like reading, listening to music, or attending cultural events positively linked those experiences with happiness (Wang and Wong 2014). In a much smaller study, researchers who studied the effects of arts-based reflection on teachers' well-being found that it helped teachers identify and express their thoughts and feelings and become more aware of the internal and external resources that support their resilience (McKay and Barton 2018). Finally, a larger review of research with adults suggests that the humanities can increase our well-being directly through rich, enjoyable, and meaningful experiences—and indirectly by fostering skills and abilities like "interpersonal connection and self- and emotion-regulation" (Westgate 2020).

An Action

I invite you to do two things this week. First, curate a small collection of valued third things—stories, case studies, poems, art, or music. Is there a lyric from a song you've always carried with you? A painting you've always loved? Perhaps nothing comes to mind yet. If not, wonderful! It's time to explore. Find at least three works of art that are meaningful to you.

Next, find a time when you might share one or more of these items with a friend, a family member, some colleagues, or even your students. And, of course, you can invite them to do the same, as time permits.

Guiding Questions

After you choose your third things, grab your journal and reflect on these prompts:

- Describe each of the items you chose.

- Why are they meaningful to you? What do they say about you?

- How would you explain their significance to colleagues or students?

After you've had the opportunity to share your third things with others, consider the following:

- How did it feel to share something meaningful to you? Briefly describe the interaction.

- What was the response?

- Did the conversation open up in ways that surprised you?

Benefits

It takes time to nurture a space for group reflection, and third things are tools for creating trust and a sense of common humanity. I still look back on my time at those retreats as formative for my personal and professional growth. They were hosted by the Center for Courage and Renewal (see Additional Resources) with a mission of creating "a more just, compassionate, and healthy world by nurturing personal and professional integrity and the courage to act on it."

When we risk revealing ourselves to others, we gain a greater sense of connection to them *and* a stronger sense of our own personal and professional identity. And art can serve as a conduit—helping us to find common ground. If "we teach who we are," as Parker Palmer reminds us, knowing and sharing ourselves with others is at the heart of our work.

Additional Resources

- Center for Courage and Renewal, https://couragerenewal.org

- Parker Palmer, "Common Ground and Third Things," https://www.youtube.com /watch?v=vEkqIBgXlOU

- Parker Palmer, *A Hidden Wholeness: The Journey Toward an Undivided Life*

Week 26: Being with Words

Educators tussle with time. Everything must be efficiently managed and scheduled—class periods, tests, phone calls, conferences—with the heartless face of the clock mocking us from the back of the classroom. The sense of urgency in our work and the rush of life can keep us from seeing and savoring what's right in front of us.

Weekends provide a respite, but Mondays can be challenging. When you fear jumping back into the fray, it can be helpful to create a quiet yet emotionally energizing "jump-start." As a teacher educator, I introduced a simple weekly ritual at my university (which continued for years). I called it "Monday Morning Musings"—a time where bleary-eyed students and professors gathered, with hot drinks in hand, to share favorite poems before class began each week (Eva et al. 2014).

A Pathway

The process was simple: we sat in a circle, listened, and quietly snapped our fingers in applause at the end of each reading. We lapped up the images and sounds of the poems together. We didn't talk about the poems we read; no analysis was needed. Students told me that our weekly get-together helped them to slow down, be consciously together, and think about things that really mattered to them. In our gatherings, the emotional fog dissipated, and we were present and attuned to the words on the page—and to each other.

Reading good poetry can be a quiet, centering act. Poetry's packaging forces us to attend. Its language, often dense with imagery, demands close and thoughtful consideration. With the music of linguistic precision, poems render the details of our lives. Poetic language can provoke new ways of seeing and knowing—and heighten our feelings of resonance with others around us.

Billy Collins, former Poet Laureate of the United States, claims that the study of poetry provides a model for learning: "When we read a poem, we enter the consciousness of another. It requires that we loosen some of our fixed notions to accommodate another point of view—which is a model of the kind of intellectual openness and conceptual sympathy that a liberal education seeks to encourage" (Collins 2001).

Research suggests that reading (and writing) poetry can enhance empathy when we're challenged to understand people different from us (Ingram 2003; Kidd and Castana 2013; Mar et al. 2009). Even classroom-based "poetry therapy" (reading poems, writing responses to them, and writing your own poems) can improve well-being and reduce anxiety, depression, and stress (Baker and Mazza 2004; Williams 2011).

I feel most alive when I slow down, attend, and appreciate the humanity around me. For these reasons, I believe that the act of reading poetry can be a form of spiritual practice. Theodore Roethke said, "You must believe that a poem is a holy thing—a good poem, that is." Reading poetry—like journaling, being outdoors, or enjoying a great meal with friends—can be spiritually sustaining. Sharon Olds maintained that "every poem is a prayer against loneliness," while W. H. Auden once stated that the essence of prayer is "to pay attention to something or someone other than oneself."

An Action

Contemplative reading is based on the medieval monastic process called *Lectio Divina*. It features deep reading (*lectio*), reflecting (*meditatio*), responding (*oratio*), and experiencing stillness and wisdom (*contemplatio*).

- Choose a short poem to read aloud. (Here are three of my favorites: "Wild Geese" by Mary Oliver, "The Guest House" by Rumi, and "Shoulders" by Naomi Shihab Nye.)

- Sit quietly for one or two minutes and relax your mind and body.

- Read slowly—and aloud—one or two phrases or lines at a time. Then pause briefly and reflect in silence.

- Continue reading and pausing in this way until you reach the end of the poem.

- To conclude, note words or phrases that stand out for you.

- Finally, end your reading with a moment of silence.

Note: If you would like to share this process with a group, consider the group practice featured on the Center for Contemplative Mind and Society's website (see Additional Resources).

Guiding Questions

After you've experimented with contemplative reading (at least once a day this week, if possible), respond to the following questions in your journal: What is it like to read a poem (or another piece of writing) slowly and deliberately? How do you benefit from this approach to reading? How might your students or colleagues benefit as well? Why?

Benefits

Sharing poems with others, as "third things," can bring us together. In his poem "A Ritual to Read to Each Other," William Stafford reminds us to always be aware of how much we don't know about others; our assumptions can lead us astray.

Literature can prompt us, as educator-humans, to *see* our students, their families, and ourselves a little differently—with sharper eyes and softer hearts—that's why I've always had a "Poetry Is Necessary" sticker on my office door. I'm a better teacher when I'm fully attuned to my students with my whole self.

Additional Resources

- Mary Keator, *Lectio Divina as Contemplative Pedagogy: Re-Appropriating Monastic Practice for the Humanities*

- "Lectio Divina," *The Center for Contemplative Mind in Society,* http://www
  .contemplativemind.org/practices/tree/lectiodivina

Week 27: Experiencing Art

When I was ten years old, I decided that I wasn't "good" at art. I remember the pride I took in adding embellishments to my calligraphy project. As my teacher walked the room, commenting on students' work, she stopped, hovered behind me, and then showered my seat-mate, Abe, with praise. I don't recall her words to me, but I remember her shrugging dismissively. I got a B- in art that year.

As a member of an artistic family, I struggle to allow myself the space to explore artmaking without hearing that voice in my head: "You're not an artist, Amy." I'm slowly learning that creativity isn't an all-or-nothing game, that I can pursue it and simply enjoy the process.

A Pathway

There's a lesson for teachers here about how important it is to foster a growth mindset in students so they feel a sense of self-efficacy as learners. There's a growing body of research pointing to the social, emotional, and academic benefits of art-based learning experiences. In fact, a large study of over ten thousand students in Texas revealed that students who participated in arts programs demonstrated more compassion, received fewer disciplinary infractions, and improved their writing scores on standardized tests (Bowen and Kisida 2020).

But let's focus on us—educators—and how *we* engage in artistic expression. If we could erase all our performance-based experiences of artmaking and consider Oscar Wilde's call to savor "art for art's sake," we might find ourselves freer to nurture our creative expression both personally and professionally, and we might experience some of the same benefits as our students.

In fact, researchers have found that artmaking enhanced positive mood when study participants practiced an open, nonjudgmental growth orientation (Futterman Collier and Wayment 2021). Specifically, they noted the importance of a "priming activity" to decrease self-focus before engaging in artmaking. In this case, adults listened to a recording encouraging them to cultivate "detached awareness": "living fully in the present with an open and non-defensive mind"—which sounds a lot like mindfulness (Wayment 2015). This research suggests that approaching artmaking as more of a contemplative practice can help us to see beyond ourselves and experience a sense of connectedness with others.

Focusing on the creative experience itself rather than the outcome also opens you up to positive emotions. On their webpage on "contemplative art," the Center for Contemplative Mind in Society says, "The *process* of making artwork is what is paramount; the work that results from the practice is not important." Contemplative art "can be especially freeing for those who feel they lack adequate artistic talent or skill, since the point of the practice is not to make 'good' art, but to observe the mind while engaging in the creative process" (see Additional Resources).

When researchers studied the use of creative reflection and contemplative artmaking with teachers, they identified several themes that emerged: the importance of connecting with others and caring for self, the value of the natural world, and the need for institutions to provide support for educator well-being (Crowder et al. 2020). In another study of a teacher-education course, graduate students reported that contemplative practices like music meditation, visualization practices, mindful movement, and journaling fostered a sense of community and collaboration, social and emotional awareness and well-being, and compassion for themselves and others (Scida and Jones 2017).

An Action

Now it's your turn to create art with contemplative awareness—a collage, a drawing, an abstract painting—or perhaps you'd like to write a poem or engage in some form of mindful dance or movement? The key here is to focus on the *process*. Before you begin, prepare yourself to be in the moment without judgment. Slow down and pay attention to your breath as you create. Become aware not just of the art itself, but also the experience of creating.

Guiding Questions

Take out your journal and reflect on the following:

- How did you feel before you began the process? What do you think and feel now?

- What was it like to enjoy creating something (rather than focusing on the final product)? Describe the experience.

- What did you learn about yourself through this process?

Benefits

Artistic engagement in all four areas of creative expression—including music engagement, visual arts therapy, movement-based creative expression, and expressive writing—can have positive effects on our stress, anxiety, and mood, and there is also evidence that art can benefit our physical health (Stuckey and Nobel 2010). And when researchers studied the effects of educators' creative mindsets on their teaching, they found that a belief in everyone's creative potential (including their own) made teachers more likely to confidently facilitate creative exploration in their classrooms (Paek and Sumners 2019).

As we engage in the creative process with greater openness and contemplative awareness, we're more likely to lose ourselves in the pleasure of creating while experiencing a sense of connectedness to others. Theologian and philosopher Meister Eckhart expresses this beautifully when he says that whatever we "take in by contemplation," we "pour out in love."

Additional Resources

- "New Studies Link the Arts to Crucial Cognitive Skills," *Edutopia,* https://www.edutopia.org/video/new-studies-link-arts-crucial-cognitive-skills

- "Contemplative Art," *The Center for Contemplative Mind in Society,* https://www.contemplativemind.org/practices/tree/contemplativeart

---

Week 28: Finding Your Creative "Flow"

Many teachers say they value creativity in the classroom, yet one study found that most rated students' creative characteristics as less desirable than other academic characteristics (Kettler et al. 2018). We see creativity's value, but we live in a world that doesn't necessarily support creative ventures—particularly in school. A lack of time, a sense of pressure, and fear of failure can stifle creativity.

Some of the elements of teaching—writing reports, grading, and standardized testing—can feel like soul-sucking activities robbing us of the agency to design meaningful learning experiences for our students. Yet teachers are fundamentally *creators*. We need to nurture that vital force to thrive.

A Pathway

According to psychologist Mihaly Csikszentmihalyi, "creativity is captured in an idea or product that is original, valued, and implemented" (2014, 162). It's also characterized as a form of divergent thinking that requires mental flexibility and originality, as well as a discovery orientation—the tendency to identify problems and formulate solutions (Runco 1991).

Remember the character-strengths assessment you took a few weeks ago? In this well-researched framework, creativity is a key strength associated with curiosity, love of learning, judgment, and perspective—all of which fall under the virtue of "wisdom" (Peterson and Seligman 2004). Other research directly links creativity with vitality and autonomy (Yu et al. 2020).

So if you want to increase your sense of creativity, begin by drawing on curiosity, a sister strength. A study of adults performing a design task reveals that curiosity was associated with more "flow"—an experience of joyful immersion in an activity—and that an increase in flow is directly related to creativity (Schutte and Malouffe 2020). Other studies of adults confirm that experiences of work-related flow predicted creativity (Zubair and Kamal 2015).

Csikszentmihalyi, who coined the term "flow," spent years studying its characteristics. After interviewing thousands of people—including artists, athletes, and ordinary people—he wanted to understand why they invested so much time and energy in the pure pleasure of activities like composing a song, conceptualizing an experiment, or designing a garden without needing an external reward. He and his team (2014) discovered that flow, as an "optimal developmental state" of absorption, features extreme concentration. Typically, the tasks that inspire flow have clear goals with automatic feedback inherent in the activities themselves. Flow can also occur when we sense that our skills match the creative challenge or opportunity in front of us. When this happens, we abandon self-consciousness and worry and simply enjoy what we're doing. We may even lose a sense of time (Csikszentmihalyi 2014).

I often find my "flow" when I write in the mornings. Sometimes I become so happily caught up in the puzzle of expressing a thought or sharing an idea that I have to rely on a 9 a.m. phone alarm to bring me back to reality when my formal workday begins. Although writing this book might not be considered as "creative" as writing a poem, I know my goal, and I have a purpose or a concept to share with you each week. As I reflect on my ideas, I'm immersed in what feels like an organic process—my words reveal themselves, and my voice emerges. Of course, writing involves steps, missteps, and revisions, but the text on the page informs me as I develop my thoughts and find my way toward coherence. Similarly, as I create learning experiences for students, I feel this same sense of movement toward clarity while exploring and discovering new ways for students to experience a particular concept or skill. It's exciting, it's rewarding, and it feeds me.

An Action

Now it's your turn. What brings you joy? Take note of the activities in your life (both personal and professional, past and present) that give you this sense of flow—of being in "the zone." Do you lose track of time when you are dancing, knitting, planting, drawing, or building something? When you're at school, do you find yourself caught up in conversations (personal or intellectual) with students or colleagues? Do you geek out on researching for a lecture or designing a new bulletin board?

Commit to carving out two brief segments of flow time (twenty to sixty minutes) for yourself in both the personal and professional realms of your life this week.

Guiding Questions

Pull out your journal and respond to the following questions:

- Which activities did you choose? Why?

- Did you experience any of the characteristics of flow (pleasure or joy; a loss of self-consciousness, worry, or sense of time)? Why or why not?

- What kind of thoughts or emotions pass through you during these activities? After these activities?

Benefits

If it hasn't struck you yet, this experience of flow directly feeds intrinsic motivation—especially when you sense opportunities for action (*That next plant goes here* or *This is just the right color for this wall*), and you feel you have the capacity or skill to respond in the moment.

The implications here are profound—for both educators and students. We may feel limited in our capacity to create at times, and that's okay. However, when we find activities that feed us—that are inherently meaningful and rewarding—we can find joy and energy and inspiration. Maya Angelou reminds us, "You can't use up creativity. The more you use, the more you have."

Additional Resources

- Mihalyi Csikszentmihalyi, *Flow: The Psychology of Optimal Experience*

- "How to Combat America's Creativity Crisis," *Greater Good,* https://greatergood
  .berkeley.edu/article/item/how_to_combat_americas_creativity_crisis

---

Exploring Your Cultural Identity

Our cultural strength has always been derived from our diversity of understanding and experience.

—Yo-Yo Ma

As an educational psychologist, I've always been intrigued about *how* we learn. Of course, *what* we learn is important, yet the complex dynamics in the classroom, the rich array of human players interacting within a "host" environment, is fascinating to me. What is the "special sauce" that carries us forward together as we explore new ideas and ways of being in the world?

You can't study the psychology of the classroom without accounting for the range of experiences and identities creating that space together. Each of us navigates multiple roles inside and outside of school—and *who we are* informs our day-to-day interactions. If you teach adolescents, this *Who am I?* question pervades everything. *Who am I* to me, and *who am I* to them? As educators, we can honor this fundamental tension with sensitivity and care.

This month, we will explore the multiple social roles and identities we navigate, how they inevitably influence our biases, and how we might bridge our perceived differences. As educators, we're the power brokers in our schools and classrooms, which requires an ongoing openness, self-inquiry, and a sense of humility as we consider our own identity tensions, biases, and the ways they play out in our relationships. This can be scary and vulnerable work, but as James Baldwin says, "Not everything that is faced can be changed, but nothing can be changed until it is faced."

Week 29: Examining Your Social Identities

When Professor Shawn Ginwright (2018) led a professional development experience at my university, he asked teachers to partner up and respond to this question: "Who are you?" As time and space opened into looming silence, the questioner in each pair continued to repeat the query: "Who *are* you?" Discomfort was palpable, yet responses became more personal after each cycle of questioning. "I'm a principal…. I'm a leader…. I'm a woman…. I'm a Black woman…. I'm a resilient trauma survivor."

You may be a teacher, an administrator, an educational consultant, or a mental health professional, but who *are* you—beyond your role at work? A review of research tells us that teacher-education programs tend to represent identity in a "unidimensional" manner—without acknowledging the complexity of our many and intersecting roles and how they influence our work (Pugach et al. 2019). We're multidimensional humans, and our competing identities influence the way we see ourselves and others.

A Pathway

A few decades ago, Henri Tajfel and John Turner (1986) described our multifaceted sense of self as our "social identity"—the sense of who we are based on group membership(s). Being part of a group can provide a sense of belonging, pride, and self-esteem, yet the notion of group membership naturally lends itself to categorization and comparison—and an "us" versus "them" orientation (Tajfel and Turner 1986).

We typically associate group memberships with things like race, age, gender, and sexuality. And when researchers interviewed a group of pre-service teachers over an academic year, they learned that teacher candidates struggled to understand and acknowledge the relationship between sexuality and race, specifically, which ultimately shaped and influenced their interactions with peers (Shelton and Barnes 2016). Further, a study of elementary school teachers' professional and social identities suggests that educators also view each other in terms of "specialty," "seniority," and "hierarchy" (Koutouzis and Spyriadou 2017).

Other studies suggest that when our social identity is threatened (particularly when we're in public and know that we're being observed), we try to reinforce our sense of self (White et al. 2018). If I'm at a party talking with someone who claims that teachers are inferior to lawyers or that my political party is ignorant of basic social issues, I'm likely to defend my affiliation or reinforce it in some way: "This is who I am and here's why."

As we become aware of the way we see ourselves—as well as the way others' see us—we also become more attuned to how our multiple identities intersect with those of our colleagues and students. In fact, researchers designed an experiment alternating the use of a mirror, a mask, and a participant's family tree to explore the complex ways that participants' current state of self-awareness fluctuated between their awareness of themselves as individuals versus their acknowledgment of their social identities (Mullen et al. 2003). How we perceive ourselves (e.g., literally through a mask, in a mirror, or through our family tree) plays out in different ways—potentially influencing our day-to-day choices and behaviors.

An Action

I invite you to identify and explore your many identities this week. Begin by brainstorming a list (socioeconomic, gender, sexual orientation, ethnicity, ability/disability, first language, age, national origin, religious or spiritual affiliation, etc.). You can also use the Social Identity Wheel as a reflection tool (see Additional Resources).

Guiding Questions

After naming each identity, respond to the following questions in your journal:

- Which identities do you think about most or least often? Why?

- Which have the strongest influence on your self-perception?

- Which have the greatest effect on how others perceive you?

- As you consider your students' and colleagues' social identities and how they might intersect with yours, what considerations come to mind?

Benefits

When we become attuned to our multiple social identities, we begin to see how they shape our experiences, beliefs, and values. Researchers argue that social identity and intersectionality are concepts at the heart of social justice education (Tapper 2013), and intersectionality is a way of understanding how aspects of a person's social identities combine to create different modes of discrimination and privilege (Crenshaw 1989). As you relate to your colleagues and students, your identities intersect with theirs and play out in complex interactions.

Teacher educators like John Powers and Beth Duffy (2016) describe ways to create "safe enough" spaces for exploring how to make our intersecting identities more visible. For example, they use theatre games to help new teachers play out identity expression and real versus ideal interactions in their classrooms. In this case, teacher candidates discovered that physically embodying various social identities and representing power dynamics in the classroom was much more memorable than reading an article or discussing a concept.

UC Berkeley professor john a. powell acknowledges this: "We are conflicted inside ourselves, which we almost never talk about, and we project that out. Part of the struggle is…getting along with different aspects of ourselves. So, this becomes not just a political or psychological journey, but a profoundly spiritual journey." And this beautiful and complicated journey requires courage and humility.

Additional Resources

- "Social Identity Wheel," LSA Inclusive Teaching: University of Michigan, https://sites.lsa.umich.edu/inclusive-teaching/social-identity-wheel

- "Social Justice Standards: Unpacking Identity," *Learning for Justice,* https://www.learningforjustice.org/professional-development/social-justice-standards-unpacking-identity

- Kimberlé Crenshaw, "The Urgency of Intersectionality," https://www.youtube.com/watch?v=akOe5-UsQ2o

Week 30: Unearthing Your Biases

In *This is Water,* David Foster Wallace shares this analogy: "There are these two young fish swimming along and they happen to meet an older fish swimming the other way, who nods at them and says, 'Morning, boys. How's the water?' And the two young fish swim on for a bit, and then eventually one of them looks over at the other and goes, 'What the hell is water?'"

I know that I swim in cultural waters that I do not see. And I don't automatically recognize the policies and systems that privilege my rights over others'. So I appreciate Robin DiAngelo's simple challenge: "Instead of asking *if* you've been shaped by these systems, ask yourself *how* you've been shaped by them" (Shapiro 2020).

If we want the best for our students, colleagues, and schools, it's crucial to acknowledge the cultural forces that shape us and to become aware of our implicit biases—"the attitudes or stereotypes that affect our understanding, actions, and decisions in an unconscious manner" (Staats 2016, 29).

Last week we explored social identities and how they shape our beliefs and behaviors. This week we'll dig a bit further to unearth some of the underlying attitudes and assumptions that inform our choices.

A Pathway

It's important to note the reality of implicit bias. Our brains process over ten million bits of information every second, and most of that processing remains outside of our awareness (Hanson 2009). It's impossible to consciously track this amount of information. Yet this flood of input can activate implicit associations or biases, which can influence our decisions. Further, when we're tired, overwhelmed, or lacking information, we default to our unconscious associations more easily.

Teachers aren't magically immune to implicit bias. Educators tend to express more positive racial attitudes when compared to non-educators (D. M. Quinn 2017). Yet when they were matched to adults with similar characteristics, researchers found that both teachers and non-teachers held explicit and implicit racial biases along with pro-white attitudes (Starck et al. 2020). Another study suggests that teachers' implicit biases vary by teacher gender and race—and that their racial bias levels were lower in counties with more Black students. However, white and Black test score and discipline disparities existed in counties where teachers scored higher on measures of racial bias (Chin et al. 2020).

Bottom line: educators' implicit racial biases can influence disparities in student achievement as well as discipline—even when Black and white students behave similarly (Van den Bergh et al. 2010; Okonofua and Eberhardt 2015). With this in mind, uncovering our implicit biases feels like imperative work. If we can detect some of our biases, we'll be more aware of how they might play out in day-to-day interactions at school.

An Action

Because implicit biases are difficult to identify, psychologists at Harvard, the University of Virginia, and the University of Washington collaboratively researched and developed a series of assessments called Implicit Association Tests, which they've tested for over twenty years. They measure participants' reaction time to pairs of images and associated words, which can indicate positive or negative biases or attitudes.

I invite you to take at least one or more of these free online assessments that measure implicit associations around race, gender, sexual orientation, and other social identities (see Additional Resources).

Guiding Questions

Although this tool may not be 100 percent valid and reliable, it may spark further thought and self-exploration. Then grab your journal and respond to the following questions:

- How did it feel to take this test? Describe your experience.

- Did you notice any thoughts or concerns rising in you before or after you saw the results?

- What did you learn about yourself?

- What further questions do you have now?

Benefits

When Patricia Clark and Eva Zygmunt (2014) studied teachers' reactions to their Implicit Association Test results, they noted five responses: disregard, disbelief, discomfort, distress, and acceptance. It's worth considering how you reacted as well. Personally, I found the scientific reality of implicit bias to be somewhat freeing. I know that I'm socialized to have biases, and I want to be aware of them so that I can actively address them.

Beyond basic awareness, there are ways we can take action to mitigate the influence of racial bias in schools: slow down and become more aware of our decision-making processes, thoughtfully review our achievement data with our colleagues, and revisit school and district policies and practices—especially around discipline (Staats 2016). This work requires an ongoing, heartfelt commitment to our students.

Additional Resources

- Harvard Implicit Association Test, https://implicit.harvard.edu/implicit/takeatest .html

- "Common Beliefs Survey: Teaching Racially and Ethnically Diverse Students," *Greater Good in Education,* https://ggie.berkeley.edu/practice/common-beliefs -survey-teaching-racially-and-ethnically-diverse-students/

Week 31: Bridging Differences

As a teacher educator, I have often asked my students to list all the fears and anxieties they remember experiencing on the first day of school. They tend to recall feelings ranging from tentative uneasiness to knee-knocking dread. One memory sometimes rises to the surface: standing with a lunch tray, cautiously scanning the filled cafeteria tables, wondering *Where should I sit? Where will I be welcome? Where do I belong?*

It's natural to look for a community—to yearn for a sense of security. We're wired for it. Yet we tend to group ourselves based on fears. *This person looks different. Am I safe here? Will these people accept me?* Beverly Tatum unpacks this self-sorting phenomenon in her book *Why Are All the Black Kids Sitting Together in the Cafeteria?* Grouping ourselves by race—or any other common identity—doesn't help us to overcome our fears about difference. At a time when racial tensions are more palpable than ever, students and teachers need to feel a sense of belonging and safety in our schools.

A Pathway

It's not shocking that biases exist—our brains respond to people from another group as if we're perceiving a *physical threat* (Wheeler and Fiske 2005). However, we can combat our wiring through perspective-taking exercises and simple stereotype-awareness activities. For example, when a group of white pre-service teachers read about their Black peers' experiences of racism and explored how they might feel and react in those situations, those teachers demonstrated less prejudice (Whitford and Emerson 2019). Teacher candidates who identified and discussed some of their common stereotypes and then engaged in an extended service-learning project demonstrated greater self-regulation around their tendency to stereotype (Pang and Park 2003).

Because our biases play out as we navigate social identities and group membership, researchers are finding that group difference is one of the greatest barriers to care and compassion for each other. We can be less motivated to help someone if they don't appear to belong to our group. In a study of soccer fans, researchers found that participants were less likely to help an injured jogger if that jogger was wearing the jersey of a rival soccer team. In another study, however, when people were prompted to consider their identity as soccer fans, they were more likely to help an injured runner wearing a soccer jersey (even of a rival team) than someone who was not wearing one (Levine et al. 2005).

The good news is that the members of our "in-group" can change. One study found that when participants focused on another person's individual preferences for vegetables more than the social categories that defined them (like their age or race), the threat activation patterns in their brains literally shifted (Wheeler and Fiske 2005). In other words, we're more open to each other when we identify basic human commonalities.

And one of the best ways to find commonalities is through "intergroup contact"—spending time with people who aren't typically part of your social group. (For example, you might join a spiritual community, advocacy organization, class, or fitness program in a different neighborhood, or invite colleagues who don't look like you to a book or film club.) This may sound simplistic, but a review of over 515 "intergroup contact" studies found that spending time together can reduce prejudice between groups relative to race, sexual orientation, disability, and mental illness. However, certain conditions need to be in place. First, you need to share a common goal. You might share a commitment to animal rights with others who volunteer at a shelter with you, or you might run with a diverse group who are all training for the same 10K race. Second, your contact with others needs to be approved by relevant authority figures like teachers, supervisors, parents, ministers, or politicians—people whose opinions matter to you (Böhm et al. 2020).

An Action

At the same time, relationships also yield conflicts and misunderstandings. If you're a human who cares in this world, you undoubtedly struggle to understand some of your colleagues or students.

On a practical level, identify someone you work with or teach. This week, take a little time to consider all the things you have in common with that person and try to identify any common goals or shared interests. (For a more detailed version of this exercise, see "Shared Identity" in Additional Resources.)

Guiding Questions

After you brainstorm a list of potential interests and goals in your journal, respond to the following questions:

- What was useful about this exercise?

- What was challenging about this exercise?

- Did this exercise shift your thinking? If so, how?

- How might this list affect your behavior the next time you interact with this person?

This simple brainstorming activity can give you a sense of possible points of connection even if you harbor some anger, fear, or hesitation about this person. It can be a helpful starting point.

Benefits

Of course, we can't bridge differences if we aren't invested in understanding and learning from each other. Students benefit—and even thrive—in racially diverse spaces. Studies indicate that academic achievement increases across race in integrated schools (Siegel-Hawley 2012). In addition, bilingual education can lead to greater academic success while enhancing students' ethnic identity, self-esteem, and self-concept (Rolstad et al. 2005).

And we're not just talking about school-wide diversity. Classroom-level integration appears to benefit students, too. In a study of over four thousand middle school students in Southern California, researchers discovered that students in racially balanced classrooms experienced greater safety, less loneliness, and less bullying. Rather than avoiding cross-race friendships with peers, they gravitated toward them (Juvonen et al. 2018). Poet Audre Lorde frames our challenge: "It is not our differences that divide us. It is our inability to recognize, accept, and celebrate those differences." When we hold and sustain welcoming spaces where our students can learn from each other, we all benefit.

Additional Resources

- "Bridging Differences Playbook," *Greater Good,* https://greatergood.berkeley.edu /images/uploads/Bridging_Differences_Playbook-Final.pdf

- "Shared Identity," *Greater Good in Action,* https://ggia.berkeley.edu/practice /shared_identity

- "Six Ways to Be an Anti-Racist Educator," *Edutopia,* https://www.edutopia .org/video/Six-ways-be-antiracist-educator

---

Week 32: Exercising Humility

Two teaching assistants of Asian ancestry walked into my office and closed the door. They had heard a white colleague make an alienating comment in class. They felt invalidated by it and worried about its impact on the students. They wanted their colleague to understand how it landed for them—and how it might be received among a culturally diverse group of students. So they approached her and made a quiet yet courageous attempt to share their feelings. Unfortunately, she breezed past their hurt and focused squarely on constructing her defense: "No, here's what I was saying. This is what I really meant."

It's so common to default to self-protection—focusing on our intent rather than the impact of what we say or do. Ideally, we pause, take a breath, and listen carefully so that we can receive the information shared and the feelings that come along with it. Unfortunately, this teacher's defensive reaction ramped up the frustration and fears her colleagues expressed.

I don't ever want to offend or hurt my students, but I also know that I probably do at times, because my racial socialization is in the air I breathe, and my perceptions as a white, heterosexual, middle-class woman can blind me to others' experiences—despite my best efforts to learn and grow.

A Pathway

Over the past decades, teachers have been navigating the rapidly changing racial and cultural demographics in schools, aspiring to achieve "cultural competence," which requires a vast knowledge of the range of needs in any given classroom or community. It's dangerous to assume that someone can possess that knowledge. "Cultural humility," as a way of being, provides a healthier, more realistic alternative. "Competence" centers around understanding how to respond to a distant "other." Yet educators with humility can acknowledge that they're part of a larger system with barriers and power differentials that require personal accountability for ongoing self-reflection (Fisher-Borne et al. 2015). In other words, educators with cultural humility would be ready and willing to understand how their words might negatively affect their students and colleagues.

Researchers describe cultural humility as both an intrapersonal and interpersonal *process.* You're aware of your limitations, knowing that you can never fully understand someone else. At the same time, you can be respectfully "other-oriented" in your daily interactions (Hook and Davis 2019). Cultural humility is also an emotional experience characterized by "mutual empowerment, respect, partnerships, optimal care, and life-long learning" (Foronda et al. 2016, 214). Teachers need to understand how their own backgrounds influence the way they might view students who differ from them.

Some teacher educators strategically embed learning experiences throughout their courses to promote both critical reflection and a sense of cultural humility. For example, Brown and her colleagues (2016) feature reflection tools including a "Biases and Stereotypes Assessment," a "Check Your Assumptions" activity based on classroom scenarios with students and families, a case study review process, and home visits with extensive family interviews.

Other programs prioritize partnerships with community agencies to facilitate service-learning experiences that can inform new teachers' understanding of themselves in relationship to their students. Teacher candidates who spend time in local communities describe the importance of "discovery through stories, care through affirming strengths, and learning through reciprocal relationships" (Tinkler and Tinkler 2016). In another service-learning study, new teachers reported an increase in self-awareness, an appreciation of immigrant children's strengths, and greater cultural humility (Lund and Lee 2015).

An Action

You may not have time to immerse yourself in another culture this week, but below you'll find tools to help you examine your humility (see Additional Resources). Take the humility survey online or in the workbook (8), then reflect on the questions below.

Guiding Questions

- You can make a conscious decision to act with humility (decisional humility), or you can experience a sense of humility on an emotional level (emotional humility). Where do you see yourself in this process?

- Which characteristics of humility come more easily for you (self-awareness, an "other" orientation, lack of superiority, etc.)?

- Which characteristics are more challenging for you?

Now that you've completed the assessment, consider a time when you were not very humble.

- Describe the event or circumstances.

- How did you feel a few days after this occurred?

- What has happened since then? Have your feelings or behaviors changed?

Note: Feel free to explore the six sections of the workbook, as time permits.

Benefits

Study participants who completed all the activities in the workbook reported an increase in humility, patience, and forgiveness—as well as an overall decrease in negativity (Lavelock et al. 2014). Of course, developing a sense of humility is a life-long journey of evolving openness, self-awareness, and self-reflection.

A sense of humility can feed our relationships with our students and colleagues as we partner together in learning. If we move away from the arrogance that we possess cultural "knowledge" and toward an enduring willingness to learn in and through relationship, our students, colleagues, and schools will benefit. "Pride makes us artificial, and humility makes us real," says Thomas Merton. If we can strip away the superficial and arrive at what is true within ourselves, we can be more "real" and alive to others.

Additional Resources

- Christine Lavelock et al., *The Path to Humility: Self-Directed Learning Workbook,* https://static1.squarespace.com/static/518a85e9e4b04323d507813b/t /533c6c0de4b047d0e06ba268/1396468749812/the-path-to-humility-six -practical-sections-for-becoming-a-more-humble-person.pdf

- "Humility Survey," http://humilityscience.com/survey

Reaching Out to Others

Strong back. Soft front. Wild heart.

—Brené Brown

You probably know a bit about how to reach out to your students. Many teachers I know have "soft fronts" and "wild hearts," but they don't always have "strong backs."

I've always struggled to find that balance. And I know that if I dutifully reach out to others without a sense of myself each day, I have less to give and less to share, so I often begin my day with a mindfulness practice that helps me with this challenge.

In "Focusing on What Matters" on YouTube, angel Kyodo williams leads you to embody a sense of your "inherent dignity" by focusing on your vertical posture as you sit and connect with the values you hold in your gut or core. Next, you slowly become more aware of the room, the people and energy around you, and your relationship to them. Strong back first—then opening to others. Vertical, then horizontal.

Feeling a sense of my own body, posture, and presence like this is one way I've learned to nurture a healthier connection to others. This month we'll explore strategies for navigating our emotional distress in the presence of others' suffering; we'll practice compassion for ourselves and others, and we'll reach out to extend kindness and the generosity of our presence to others.

Month

9

Week 33: Understanding Empathic Distress

I've always been pretty good at reading the energy in a room. Problem is—I *feel* it in my body, and I tend to carry it with me. Can you relate? Psychologist Daniel Goleman (2006) explains that we all have a "neural wi-fi system" for picking up the social signals around us.

You walk into a party and sense the positive energy. You enter the staff meeting a minute late and wonder what was just said, because the tension is palpable—you can almost taste it. You see a colleague across the room in deep emotional pain, and you feel a visceral sense of that pain in your own body. Despite your care for them, you can't help them if you're suffering, too.

Empathy—the capacity to "feel with" and understand others' emotions—connects us with each other. At the same time, it can be heart-wrenching, sometimes even unbearable. And some of us are more susceptible to "emotional contagion," the tendency to automatically adopt the emotional state of another person (Bernhardt and Singer 2012).

Quite honestly, I've struggled with empathic overwhelm for years, as both a teacher and as a mother, so this topic is close to my heart. Thankfully, I now have more practical tools for regulating my distress, which I'd like to share with you. With time, practice, and greater self-awareness, you can learn to navigate your emotional distress so that you can reach out from a position of strength.

A Pathway

To begin, it's important to acknowledge our human wiring. Brain-imaging studies tell us that a person experiencing pain and someone empathizing with it can share similar brain-activation patterns (Lamm et al. 2011). No wonder some of us struggle at the sight of others' suffering. Our empathic responses can take one of two neural pathways—toward "empathic distress" or "empathic concern."

When people experience empathic distress, they tend to focus on their own negative feelings, often leading to avoidance, burnout, and poor health. However, people who experience empathic concern can separate and manage their personal feelings in the face of others' pain, opening them up to more positive emotions, a desire to help, and better health outcomes (Klimecki and Singer 2011). In fact, people who experience empathic concern also tend to demonstrate greater generosity through things like charitable giving (Ashar et al. 2017).

Psychological distancing seems to be key to navigating emotional turmoil and shifting from empathic distress to concern. There are many ways to step back and adopt a more detached perspective, and two of them we've already practiced: identifying and labeling your emotions and challenging your thoughts (week 1 and week 19). However, there are also other ways to remove yourself from the immediate situation and adopt a different perspective:

- *Visualize an observer.* It could be a fly on the wall, a thoughtful friend, or a role model. Consider how this outside observer might advise you.

- *Avoid using the pronoun "I."* When you use third-person pronouns to describe a situation, you remove yourself from the center of the story ("I was overwhelmed" vs. "She was overwhelmed").

- *Write about the distressing situation.* As you put pen to paper and flesh out a narrative description, you inevitably "step back" to frame the event.

- *Focus on your future self.* During a challenging time, ask yourself, "How would I feel about this one week from now or ten years from now?"

An Action

Recall a time when it was difficult for you to be with a suffering colleague, student, friend, or family member. Now, choose at least *two* of the four strategies above to create some psychological distance as you reflect on that time.

Guiding Questions

Pull out your journal and describe the event.

- What happened? How did you feel in your body? What thoughts did you have? What did you do in that moment?

- Now step back from the event itself and reframe it. Choose one of the strategies above and try it. Then try a second strategy.

- Which psychological-distancing tool seems more effective for you? Why? How might you use it the next time you're caught up in your own distress?

Benefits

Researchers found that the four self-distancing strategies above proved effective in helping people to manage their distress. In fact, in one "visualizing an observer" study, five-year-olds who imagined Batman in the situation and asked themselves, *What would Batman do?* were able to self-distance more effectively (White and Carlson 2015). Shifting pronouns, using expressive writing, and imagining a future self (temporal distancing) are also helpful tools for reframing and contextualizing a difficult event (Bruehlman-Senecal and Ayduk 2015; Kross et al. 2014; Park et al. 2016).

However, the most evidence-based and beneficial strategy of all is learning how to practice and *experience* compassion, the feeling that arises when you perceive another's suffering and feel motivated to relieve that suffering (Goetz et al. 2010).

Additional Resources

- "How to Avoid the Empathy Trap," *Greater Good,* https://greatergood.berkeley .edu/article/item/how_to_avoid_the_empathy_trap

- "How Empathic Are You?," *Greater Good,* https://greatergood.berkeley.edu /quizzes/take_quiz/empathy

---

Week 34: Responding with Compassion

At the end of my best friend's five-year battle with cancer, I sat beside her a lot—during chemo, on the porch swing, on the couch, and next to her bed. I sat bearing witness to deep physical and psychological pain, knowing there was little I could do to ease her suffering. At times I felt tossed around in an emotional tailspin myself, searching for the presence of mind to be there for her. Over time, I learned that the best way for me to self-soothe and calm my own distress was through a compassion-based mindfulness practice.

There are strategies and tools to help us detach from our own distress—including ways to cognitively reframe a situation—and then there are experiences or ways of being that we can practice and learn to embody.

A Pathway

Last week we explored the dangers of empathic distress, which is inevitably self-focused and can trap us in our heads and bodies. However, when we feel empathic concern, also known as compassion, we're likely to feel more grounded, present, and able to respond to someone who needs us.

Compassion is the feeling that arises when you perceive another's struggle and want to lessen their suffering. It's empathy plus the desire to help (Goetz et al. 2010). And the good news is that we can train our brains to respond more compassionately. There are mindfulness practices that encourage people to experience compassion toward themselves, their family and friends, "neutral" people (like strangers), and even people we don't particularly like.

When researchers studied the brain activity of long-time meditators as they considered someone else's suffering, they discovered that the care, connection, and compassion brain networks were activated—rather than the empathic distress pathways (Lutz et al. 2008). A review of multiple studies also tells us that mindfulness and "loving-kindness" practices, in which you mentally send good wishes to others, can help us to generate greater compassion (Luberto et al. 2018). You can extend love and kindness by wishing peace, safety, health, and happiness for a student, colleague, or your boss.

You've already learned that cognitive reappraisal—shifting or reframing your interpretation of an event—can help you navigate stress. However, compassion practices may be more effective at helping us maintain a sense of care as we face others' pain. When Helen Weng and her colleagues (2018) studied people's brains as they viewed images of human suffering, they discovered that participants with two weeks of compassion practice could focus on those visual images longer and with less amygdala activation than participants with two weeks of cognitive-reappraisal training. In fact, people who practiced compassion were less emotionally reactive to those images.

An Action

If you're struggling to support a suffering friend, colleague, or student—or weighed down by the suffering in the world—try breathing in compassion for yourself and breathing out compassion for the suffering person or people. It's a practice that helps you—in the moment—to find balance and a sense of peace (see Additional Resources for one version).

Guiding Questions

After trying this practice, respond to the following questions in your journal:

- What did it feel like to breathe in compassion for yourself and breathe out compassion for others? Did you notice any shifts in your body sensations? Thoughts? Feelings?

- Were there any particular words or phrases from the practice that resonated for you?

- How do you feel now?

Benefits

Compassion-cultivation techniques like this one can increase positive emotions and a sense of social connection, lessen distress at human suffering, and reduce people's fears of feeling compassion for others in the first place (Condon et al. 2013; Klimecki et al. 2013). Compassion can also bolster resilience and improve relationships. It's associated with greater happiness, increased immune response in the face of stress, and a decrease in worry (Jazaieri et al. 2014; Leiberg et al. 2011; Pace et al. 2009).

There's an emotional letting-go that must happen in situations where suffering is beyond our control. We can tilt at windmills, worry, and ruminate. If we love someone dearly, we want to alleviate their suffering, and sometimes there is little to be done. But we can take deep breaths. Sit beside them. *Be* with them.

When Lisa was dying, I regularly drew on this compassion practice as I sat beside her. Despite my struggle with empathic distress, this practice calmed me. She, too, expressed a sense of peace and deep gratitude as she fell into a "simplicity of being" that felt emotionally healing for her. When I think about Lisa and the last few months of her life, I picture us sitting quietly together, holding that sacred space.

Additional Resources

- Tara Brach, *Radical Compassion*

- "Breathing Compassion In and Out," *Mindful Magazine,* https://www.mindful.org /breathing-compassion-in-and-out

- "Loving-kindness for Adults," *Greater Good in Education,* https://ggie.berkeley .edu/practice/loving-kindness-for-adults

Week 35: Practicing Kindness

I get a little uncomfortable talking about "kindness." Maybe it's because of my religious upbringing—I mastered the art of "good girl" performances. Maybe it's because it feels like "kindness" is a sort of surface-level, drop-in-the-bucket, sometimes disingenuous way of being. And now I notice my anger seeping through as I write this.

I can't help bumping up against the feeling that "kindness," as I was taught it, is too sweet and benign to affect a world weighed down by racial injustice, political conflicts, and profound psychological trauma. "Niceness" isn't enough to heal us. Yet things like empathy, compassion, and kindness are profoundly valuable, soft-yet-fierce qualities, because they can guide us to see each other more clearly, communicate more effectively with one another, and help us to navigate real conflicts and tensions in school and beyond.

Of course, it's one thing to feel empathy or even compassion, and another to actually reach out and help each other. As educators, we may not have the power to make everything better, but there are some things we can do—and many that we're already doing.

A Pathway

No doubt you were drawn to education because of your compassion—your desire to contribute to something larger than yourself and to help. Like compassion, kindness includes the intention to benefit other people, but a kind act may entail some cost or risk to ourselves. It may require some form of personal sacrifice of time, energy, or money. And it doesn't necessarily connote a sweet, gentle act. It's powerful stuff.

Despite the cost, there are many ways you already engage in kind or helpful behaviors, some of which might not even be on your radar. You may volunteer at a food bank or animal shelter or donate to children in poverty. Or maybe you're the person at work who always remembers your colleagues' birthdays and rallies the troops to put together a beautiful card. Regardless of how you help people outside of your immediate circle, your career choice alone reflects your wiring for connection.

Our biology can bring us together and fuel kindness. You've already learned about the empathy circuitry in our brains that tracks and senses others' pain (Lamm et al. 2011). Researchers also link the hormone oxytocin with cooperation, teamwork, and trust (Bartz et al. 2011). Also known as the "moral molecule" or the "cuddle hormone," we produce oxytocin when we reach out to each other through a gentle, reassuring touch or a gesture of support.

And then there is the vagus nerve, a major channel of our calming, "rest and digest" parasympathetic nervous system, meandering its way through our bodies. When this nerve is activated, it lowers your heart rate and blood pressure and even helps to regulate the relationship between breathing and calming. If you wonder why human connection can feel good, the vagus nerve may be part of the answer. Apart from these health benefits, research links the vagus nerve with positive emotions, compassion, and social engagement (Porges 2011).

At times it may feel costly to invest time and energy in others (we have only so much), but the rewards are huge, both to the people we help and to us. When we tap into our wiring and become more alive to each other's needs, we experience a more joyful, meaningful life.

In this moment, you may feel that you already give enough and that much of your invisible labor at home and at school goes unnoticed—and that may be true. If so, I encourage you to become more aware of the ways you give and enjoy savoring those moments. Or you may feel somewhat isolated and disconnected from others. If so, research tells us that performing random acts of kindness can improve your well-being (Curry et al. 2018).

An Action

Choose one thing to do for a colleague and one thing for a student this week. You might bring your colleague their favorite hot drink in the morning, cover their recess or lunch duty, or send them a note of appreciation. A student might benefit from some extra time—encouragement and attention during a lunch break, a visit to their soccer match, or focused time listening to them describe their favorite hobby. Enjoy reaching out and acknowledging these two special people this week.

Guiding Questions

As you reflect on your experience, answer the following questions in your journal:

- Describe your two acts of kindness. Why did you choose them?

- How did your colleague and student respond?

- How did these acts of kindness make you feel?

Benefits

When you take the time to reflect on acts of kindness, you feel happier (Otake et al. 2006). Kindness can also improve your physical and mental health. For example, volunteer work has been linked to lowered blood pressure and depression (Hopper 2016; Musick and Wilson 2003). And when our students practice kindness, they may also experience benefits to their well-being, academic achievement, social competence, peer acceptance, and school engagement (Caprara et al. 2000; Datu and Park 2019; Flook et al. 2015; Layous et. al 2012; Scheier et al. 2013).

According to multiple studies, when we demonstrate kindness or model helpful, prosocial actions, there can be a clear ripple effect (Jung et al. 2020). And in schools, kindness and a sense of school connectedness can ultimately reduce aggression and conflict. Consider the words of Maya Angelou in her poem "Continue," encouraging us to keep astonishing a mean world with our acts of kindness.

Additional Resources

- Jamil Zaki, *The War for Kindness: Building Empathy in a Fractured World*

- "Teaching and Learning for the Greater Good," *Greater Good Science Center,* https://greatergood.catalog.instructure.com/courses/teaching-and-learning -for-the-greater-good-2

- "Making Kinder Classrooms and Schools," *Greater Good in Education,* https://ggie.berkeley.edu/practice/making-kinder-classrooms-and-schools

---

Week 36: Taking Pleasure in Generosity

Yesterday I met a retired woman on Whidbey Island near Seattle—a spot where I dream of living someday. As I walked by her house, she paused and turned off her lawn mower just to say hi. She went on to praise the mower and the neighbor who had just loaned it to her. We chatted for a few minutes about city life in Seattle versus island life, and she raved about the sense of community she feels in her town. "People help older folks with house repairs and landscaping if they need it, and the town has emergency funds ready to go for anyone in a pinch."

I live in Seattle, where people are often isolated and frenzied. Most people pass each other on sidewalks without acknowledgment. "Why is it so different in the city?" I asked my new friend. "Is it about greed?" She paused, teared up, and said, "It's time. People don't want to invest time in each other."

A Pathway

The pace of life in schools seems to parallel city life. Educators identify an ongoing sense of "time pressure" as one of the key stressors they face at work (Jennings et al. 2013). However, there are quiet, simple things we can do to respond to our communities' needs.

Perhaps you balk at the idea of extending generosity to others when you invest so much in your students already. However, giving can make you feel better, too. When we practice generosity, the reward circuits in our brains light up just as they would when we eat good food or experience sexual intimacy. This biological phenomenon suggests that doing good is important to our survival as a species. In fact, one study found that even people forced to give money to others showed an increase in "feel good" neural activity, although people's reward-based pathways were even stronger when they volunteered their own funds (Harbaugh et al. 2007).

Imagine you have a $10 gift card to your local coffee shop. Would it make you happiest if you were told to spend it on yourself (with a friend present), give it to someone else, or treat someone else to coffee with your card? Lara Aknin and her team (2011) discovered that participants who shared their card and their time with someone else reported feeling happiest. It's rewarding to give, and it's also deeply gratifying to share an experience of giving.

WEEK 36

Theoretically, this all sounds wonderful to me. However, while I support charities financially, I struggle to find time to give to others, so I'm learning to slow down and make giving more of a conscious practice. Fortunately, there are several things we can do to encourage ourselves and our colleagues reach out and give.

First, research indicates that we tend to respond with more generosity and care if we're cued to acknowledge human connectedness (Pavey et al. 2011). We can post quotes in our classrooms about the importance of community and shared purpose, or decorate hallways with pictures of warm and loving gestures of friendship. Simple environmental cues can spark greater generosity and kindness at school.

In addition, our capacity for generosity also depends on how we view others' suffering and whether we feel empowered to help. When we learn of one person's struggle rather than stats about a larger social problem, we're more likely to help. When people read a story of one girl living in poverty, they're more likely to donate to an anti-hunger charity than those who read statistics about poverty (Small et al. 2007). Finally, when we reflect on how our generosity might benefit someone else, and we choose how we want to help, we're more likely to experience greater well-being (Aknin et al. 2013; Weinstein and Ryan 2010).

An Action

This week, rather than sending money to a charity, consider if there's someone in your community who might benefit more directly from your time and generosity. Choose one small way to support that person this week. Could you drive them to an appointment or help with an errand? Or drop by for a brief visit with flowers, or go for a walk together and talk?

Guiding Questions

After you've given to someone in your community, grab your journal and reflect on the experience.

- Describe your gift. How was it received?

- What does it feel like to give time versus money?

- Did you notice any shifts in your emotions, thoughts, or behaviors before, during, or after this experience?

Benefits

When we expand our notion of generosity to include giving time—not just money—it looks a lot like kindness. Savoring another person's joy can be incredibly meaningful, and generous acts, in their many forms, can improve both our physical and mental health (S. Allen 2018b). Even better, generosity can be socially contagious. Watching someone else give can prime others to do the same (Nook et al. 2016).

My friend on Whidbey Island knew in her gut what research tells us: giving to each other—especially our time—is powerful stuff. I want to be more attuned to those moments when I can reach out with my heart.

Additional Resources

- "Reminders of Connectedness," *Greater Good in Action,* https://ggia.berkeley .edu/practice/reminders_of_connectedness

- "Putting a Face on Human Suffering," *Greater Good in Action,* https://ggia .berkeley.edu/practice/putting_a_human_face_on_suffering

---

MONTH 10

Growing Your Relationships

Each friend represents a world in us, a world not born until they arrive, and it is only by this meeting that a new world is born.

—Anaïs Nin

One of the things that surprised me most about my first year of teaching high school was how lonely I felt, despite teaching 163 students per day. Outside of the classroom, I lived in my own private world, spinning on each day's events. I rarely joined my colleagues at lunch. I was just trying to keep up with everything. I avoided the very connections I craved.

With the rush and overwhelm of our days, we need each other. Even when time is short, we can savor the moments we share. This month we'll focus on nurturing simple connections, learning to slow down and communicate more effectively, listen to others' perspectives, and share in their joy.

Week 37: Communicating Mindfully

A global pandemic, intensifying racial conflicts, and political polarization—these challenges feed into the angry, reactive communication that floods social media, seeps into our meetings, and charges up our face-to-face conversations. As educators, we know that effective communication is the foundation of our work, yet we face growing tensions all around us.

Most of us tend to focus on the "what" in a difficult conversation. "What will I say next?" "What is my best argument?" "Why don't they get it? This is infuriating!" Caught up in the words, we lose each other. So let's focus on the "how" this week.

A Pathway

There is one thing we can control—what we bring to a conversation or interaction. Earlier we learned about mindfulness, but here's where it gets interesting. You may practice mindfulness in the comfort of your home or office, and I have for years, but learning to draw on those skills throughout a difficult conversation takes time and focus—and humility.

Researchers measure "interpersonal mindfulness"—your mindful awareness during social interactions—through a survey that targets three key mindfulness components: nonjudgmental presence, awareness of self and others, and nonreactivity (Medvedev et al. 2020). For example, can you listen to another person without judging or criticizing them (or yourself)? Are you aware of the tone of your voice or the other person's body language and facial expression? Are you aware of your own feelings without being overtaken by them?

A recent study links some of the key facets of mindfulness with both empathy and active listening (Jones et al. 2019). If you're mindfully aware of yourself and others during an interaction, you're more likely to slow down and figuratively step outside of a conversation to observe and describe what is happening. And if you're nonreactive and nonjudgmental of yourself and others, no doubt you'll demonstrate more empathy and be genuinely open to listening.

In fact, when college students described their biggest disappointment at school with trained listeners, they preferred "active" and aware listeners (who paraphrased their words and asked them to elaborate) over advice givers, and listeners who offered simple acknowledgments like a head nod, "I see," or "Okay" (Weger et al. 2014).

Oren Sofer outlines several key skills for enhancing "relational awareness" in his book on mindful communication. If you're relationally aware, you develop a "balance of inner and outer awareness" (2018, 54), and you learn to navigate the flow of the conversation with greater intentionality.

An Action

During your interactions this week, try to focus more on the "how" rather than the "what" by developing an awareness of how your interactions flow. Choose one or more of the following skills of awareness that Sofer (2018) describes and notice how they influence your conversations:

- Choice points: observe moments when you can choose to listen or to speak.

- Pausing: practice slowing down and taking longer versus shorter pauses in conversation.

- Pace: adjust your speaking pace to become more aware of how you're speaking.

Guiding Questions

As you experiment with the flow of your conversations, record your thoughts.

- Did you notice times when it was better to focus on your conversation partner's words or did you find yourself needing to speak?

- What did it feel like to practice pausing? How did that affect the conversational flow?

- What did you notice about the pace of your speech or your partner's speech? How did it affect the conversation?

- Does focusing on the "how" feel artificial? If so, why? What did you learn about yourself?

Benefits

Mindfulness and active listening can go hand in hand in promoting empathy, which can lead to greater connection, understanding, and trust. And a large review of studies indicates that mindfulness skills play a role in weakening the biases we hold against other groups of people (Oyler et al. 2021).

In fact, interpersonal mindfulness skills correlate with friendship or relationship quality (Pratscher et al. 2018). And leaders who demonstrate a mindful communication style at work have staff members who feel more content and satisfied with their leadership (Arendt et al. 2019). Even students believe that their own ability to listen well contributes to their academic and future success (Eggenberger 2021). Rather than simply focusing on what we say to each other, it's worth investing more in how we bring ourselves into the conversation. We can learn to slow down and hold spaces for listening—to ourselves and each other.

Additional Resources

- Oren Sofer, *Say What You Mean: A Mindful Approach to Nonviolent Communication*

- "How Mindful Communication Makes Us More Compassionate," *Mindful Magazine,* https://www.mindful.org/stop-go-wait

---

Week 38: Putting Yourself in Others' Shoes

"I know exactly how you feel," said a colleague, as they breezed past my hurt to chronicle their own harrowing story. I found myself emotionally forlorn and unheard. Yet I'm sometimes guilty of doing the same thing. In my eagerness to reach out to others, I've caught myself even *interrupting* them to let them know how much I "understand" and "care." Ouch.

Skills like empathy connect us with others. And perspective-taking, the cognitive component of empathy, can be a relationship-building tool, helping us understand others by placing ourselves in their shoes. Yet research tells us that perspective-taking can be faulty, because it's inevitably infused with our own thoughts and feelings. That smile on your student's face may be expressing awkward discomfort rather than joy, and your colleague's seemingly angry body language might reflect exhaustion. One review of twenty-five studies in this area concludes that perspective-taking should be called "perspective-mistaking," because participants across studies often made inaccurate assumptions about others (Eyal et al. 2018).

A Pathway

Researchers differentiate two forms of perspective-taking. First, we imagine self as the other. Second, we simply imagine the other (Batson et al. 1997). Apparently, when you focus purely on imagining the other, you're more intentional about letting go of your own opinions, values, and default ways of thinking. In other words, you attempt to lose your ego, which isn't always easy to do. To further complicate things, we tend to empathize more with people who are part of our social group—not outside of it (Levine et al. 2005). So empathy has its limits.

We have explored the danger of empathic distress in a previous week, and now we're acknowledging that humans' so-called understanding or perspective-taking abilities may not be accurate or selfless. After forty years of study, Daniel Batson claims that feeling empathy for a person may very well lead to helping that person (Batson et al. 2005), but several factors may get in the way. For example, empathy and compassion may be challenged during high levels of conflict, when the level of trust across groups is low, and when there are tricky power dynamics involved.

In *The Power Paradox,* psychologist Dacher Keltner (2016a) reviews a range of studies that ultimately suggest this: when we have more money and power, our capacity for empathy declines. Empathy can deepen and even perpetuate power differentials and can shift dangerously toward pity and condescension—or even domination. With this in mind, we should examine the power structures in our schools and consider how they might influence or limit opportunities for empathy, compassion, and connection.

In fact, if you hold the power in a conflict, it's best to simply listen rather than assume you know what others are thinking or feeling. In one study of perspective-taking as a tool to resolve group conflict (with Palestinians vs. Israelis, and Mexican immigrants vs. white residents of Arizona), researchers determined that people who are frequently marginalized benefit most from *sharing* their perspective rather than having someone "take" their perspective (Bruneau and Saxe 2012).

The takeaway here is this—it's best to focus on perspective-*receiving* rather than perspective-*taking*. Exercise humility; don't make assumptions based on your limited, self-constructed understanding; engage in conversation; ask a lot of questions and open yourself up to really listen.

An Action

Chezare Warren's (2018) research in classrooms indicates that culturally responsive empathy features two components. First, educators commit to engaging in "imagine other" perspective-taking through classroom activities, check-ins, and other rituals that help them gain knowledge of their students. Second, educators actively respond and adapt to their students' ongoing feedback.

This week, practice perspective-taking in the "imagine other" mode. Then, gather additional information or ask questions to determine what your student (or colleague) is really feeling or experiencing.

Guiding Questions

- As you consider your recent perspective-taking efforts, describe how you attempted to imagine what someone else was thinking and feeling?

- Were your assumptions correct?

- What methods helped you to explore this person's perspective? What did you learn? How will you respond?

Benefits

Despite cognitive empathy's limits, a review of studies links empathy with reduced racial bias, more kind and helpful behaviors, effective communication and conflict resolution, and stronger relationships within and between social groups (Klimecki 2019; Todd et al. 2011).

Perhaps not surprisingly, students claim that empathy is one of the qualities they value most in their teachers (Branwhite 1988). And when our students practice empathy themselves, they demonstrate greater academic engagement and experience stronger, kinder, more inclusive relationships at school (Santos et al. 2011; Spinrad and Eisenberg 2009).

Additional Resources

- "What Happens When You Tell Your Story and I Tell Mine?" *Greater Good*, https://greatergood.berkeley.edu/article/item/What_Happens_When_You_Tell _Your_Story_and_Tell_Mine

- "Active Listening for School Staff," *Greater Good in Education,* https://ggie .berkeley.edu/practice/active-listening-for-school-staff/#tab__1

Week 39: Feeling Empathic Joy

My first observation of Jeremy was rough. As a student teacher, he was continually redirecting the middle schoolers in his language arts class. It felt like a verbal game of whack-a-mole: "Louis, sit down." "Lashonda, your pencil is sharpened; go back to your seat, please." "Eric and William, stop talking."

Little pockets of chaos and distraction kept emerging, and Jeremy was trying to address them—one after the next. New teachers' number-one fear tends to be whether they can manage a classroom, and this task required Jeremy's full focus for the hour that I watched him. As a result, the actual writing lesson he wanted to teach inevitably spiraled down on his priority list.

So I sat down with him to discuss what happened, and we decided to test the waters with a complete change in his focus.

A Pathway

It's easy to feel threatened as a new teacher (and as a human being, for that matter). It's also common to notice and remember the negative (comments, behaviors). We're wired to respond to potential threats—and to be self-protective when emotions are high. We're also inevitably attuned to what is wrong in the world (or in our classroom). So when a student's behavior is different, unfamiliar, or unanticipated, how do we respond?

Perhaps one of the most important things we can do is to check our lens. Paul Gorksi (2011) says that "the most devastating brand of…deficit thinking emerges when we mistake difference—particularly difference from ourselves—for deficit." And psychologist Shawn Ginwright (2018) urges us to move *beyond* deficit thinking to a more "healing-centered" response: *What is right? Do I see your strengths? Do you see them? How can you use them right now?* In fact, students respond when we deliberately shift our lens from the negative to the positive.

When researchers observed over twelve hundred (primarily white) teachers in the United States who worked in ethnically diverse schools, they found that teachers' "empathic joy"—or "positive empathy"—played a powerful role in their classrooms (Pittinsky and Montoya 2016). Empathic joy turns the traditional concept of empathy on its head. Although empathy generally connotes feeling or understanding someone else's suffering or struggles, empathic joy is the experience of sharing and understanding positive emotions. When our students feel happy, we feel happy. When our students experience a success ("I did it!"), we revel in that success along with them. As the Swedish proverb goes, "Shared joy is double joy."

So why not delight in the good this week? Focus on empathic joy and feel your students' positive emotions.

An Action

This week, choose at least one way to recognize and acknowledge your students' positive emotions and experiences. Record and celebrate moments that you enjoyed observing—one student high-fiving a friend after finishing a group task, or another persevering in solving a math problem—whatever inspires you. For example, you might leave notes on your students' desks each day or send postcards home to families that highlight students' positive emotions and actions and how they made you feel. Alternatively, you might incorporate an end-of-day (or class period) ritual of recognition in which you and your students acknowledge moments of growth or positive connection. Bottom line: choose an approach that feels meaningful to you—one where you can recognize and savor vicarious experiences of joy.

Guiding Questions

Before you launch into the action above, recall a few times when you shared in the joy of your students (e.g., eyes that brightened with understanding? The eager chatter of a small group of students raring to go before a debate? The glow on a student's face after receiving that college acceptance letter?). When and how did you experience empathic joy? Where? With whom? Did your student(s) sense that you were celebrating with them? How did they know?

Benefits

Researchers Todd Pittinsky and R. Matthew Montoya (2016) found that when teachers acknowledged, modeled, and encouraged affirming interactions among students of different races, ethnicities, genders, and abilities, student achievement increased. Expressing empathic joy in the classroom can be transformative—not only for enhancing academic success, but also for fostering a healthier school climate, as well as improved life outcomes for students. In fact, researchers connect positive empathy with personal well-being, a sense of social closeness, and kind and helpful (prosocial) behaviors (Morelli et al. 2015).

Let's go back to my student teacher Jeremy. He slowly shifted classroom dynamics by adjusting his lens and experiencing the good things happening each day. As he basked in his students' individual mini-joys and accomplishments, he channeled that positive energy back out to the whole group—acknowledging and praising his students, rather than continuously correcting them. His students' energy and engagement grew. It didn't happen overnight, but it happened.

Additional Resources

- Barbara Fredrickson, *Positivity: Discover the Upward Spiral That Will Change Your Life*

- "How to Overcome Stress by Seeing Other People's Joy," *Greater Good,* https://greatergood.berkeley.edu/article/item/how_to_overcome_stress_by _seeing_other_peoples_joy

---

Week 40: Sustaining Connections

My most vivid memory of my first year as a high school teacher is one of isolation. Me—lying on the floor of my office at lunchtime, door locked, lights out—alone and overwhelmed.

New teachers can be the most susceptible to stress—largely because they tend to struggle with unrealistic expectations of themselves. Rather than reaching out for help, their primary strategy for stress management is hunkering down and working harder (Skaalvik and Skaalvik 2015), which is why I found myself stretched out on a concrete floor facing burnout in my first year of teaching. I've always been good at caring for others, yet one thing I struggled with (and sometimes still do) is how to ask for help.

A Pathway

We're other-focused on our resilience journey this month, but let's check in with ourselves again. Educators tend to give and give, so reaching out on our own behalf is crucial to our resilience. During my first year as a high school teacher, I had no formal mentor, few visits from colleagues, and one formal evaluation from my principal. The sense of alienation, loneliness, and driving perfectionism that knocked me down that year eventually led me to become a teacher educator, mindfulness practitioner, and educational psychologist who focuses on adult social and emotional well-being.

That year I learned that I simply could not face my workload alone. I needed support. Social support is the experience of being cared for, valued, and part of a mutually supportive human network (S. E. Taylor 2011). Research tells us that social support plays a role in lessening the impact of job demands and emotional exhaustion on teachers (Kinman et al. 2011).

In his book *Together,* Vivek Murphy explains how we humans evolved to need and belong to each other, and he highlights the three different categories of connection that provide meaning and value in our lives: the intimate (a partner), the relational (friends), and the collective (community). (See Additional Resources.)

At this point, it's worth taking stock of your people. If you don't have a roommate, spouse, or partner, who is in your "friend" network (inside or outside of work), and how do you connect with larger communities—whether you're a part of a support group, a faith-based community, a kickball league, or a book club? Personally, I tend to forget who is available for a call, a joke, a walk, or a Zoom conversation, so I find it helpful to map out the web of people I know and trust in my journal or to stick a reminder note near my computer ("Don't forget to call Kerri" or "Zoom with Kira on Friday"). If you're struggling to identify people to talk to, however, it may be worth considering a yoga class or a teacher support group. You can form one yourself.

And as you map out the network of humans in your life, take note of the ways in which they support you. Researchers Carolyn Cutrona and Julia Suhr (1992) identified the following categories of social support:

- Informational support: advice or feedback (e.g., people you can ask, "How should I handle this teaching challenge?")

- Emotional support: sympathy, empathy, and an understanding of your experience ("No wonder you're stressed right now! I get it.")

- Esteem support: recognition of your skills and abilities through compliments and validation ("You've got this—you're a strong leader with a lot of grit.")

- Social network support: accessible, online community-based resources, including discussion forums and people available to check in and chat about your interests or dilemmas ("We're here for you! Share your questions and comments here.")

You may have casual, fun friends, or people who give helpful advice or who come through for you when you're down. With your revised list or network of specialized supporters in mind, note how many are work colleagues. Research tells us that teachers' working relationships at school can be more effective at preventing burnout than social support outside of school (Fiorilli et al. 2019).

An Action

Friendships can give us greater purpose and meaning, better health outcomes, and even longer lives (Denworth 2020). However, when you're busy, they take planning as well as a commitment to show up.

This week, take a few minutes each day to reach out to at least one person (a text, email, phone date, or a cup of tea or coffee). In addition, make a commitment to nurture one specific relationship over the coming month. Schedule time to meet (online, by phone, or in person).

Guiding Questions

Now, reflect on the following questions in your journal:

- Who did you choose to connect with during the week and across the month? Why?

- What did you notice in yourself before, during, and after you reached out?

- What will you keep in mind as you nurture one relationship over the next month?

Benefits

A review of studies links social support with physical and health benefits, including less depression and anxiety under stress, better adjustment to chronic health conditions, less cognitive decline, and lower mortality rates (Taylor 2011). Schools can play a role in fostering a sense of belonging and social support. When teachers strongly identify with their school and feel a sense of teamwork, they tend to perceive a reduced workload, which lowers stress (Avanzi et al. 2018). Beyond your school, large, energized teacher support programs continue to grow—take heart; you're not alone. Have the courage to reach out.

Additional Resources

- Vivek Murphy, *Together: The Healing Power of Human Connection*

- Happy Teacher Revolution, https://www.happyteacherrevolution.com

- "Social Capital Quiz," *Greater Good,* https://greatergood.berkeley.edu/quizzes /take_quiz/social_capital

---

Nurturing Supportive Spaces

Trauma is disconnection from ourselves.

—Gabor Maté

This month we acknowledge our human need for safety, belonging, and healing in a world where trauma is pervasive. However, rather than jumping right into the science of trauma—the triggers, the signs, the symptoms—let's begin by acknowledging that the effects of trauma are deeply personal, very real, and very human. If trauma is fundamentally "disconnection from ourselves," how comforting it can be to find ourselves again in a safe space where we're seen and acknowledged.

"I see you. Everyone matters." Mindfulness scholar Rhonda Magee (2019) recommends using this refrain to begin a class or meeting. She suggests standing in a circle and, if it's comfortable for you, looking into the eyes of everyone in the room. You can offer others a smile or simply honor each person in the room with quiet, respectful attention. Research tells us that we're more resilient when we feel socially connected and supported—when we're in relationship.

Week 41: Acknowledging Trauma

Students walk into our schools with a range of histories, experiences, and traumas—and so do we. Gabor Maté, author of *In the Realm of Hungry Ghosts,* says, "I think normalcy is a myth…. The idea that some people have pathology and the rest of us are normal is crude." And because we're all interconnected through a shared human history, we can also experience a sense of collective trauma. Trauma affects everyone—directly or indirectly—whether we experience threats to our relationships, to our public health, or to our environment. If we want to foster safe, supportive spaces for learning and growing, we must begin by acknowledging the reality of widespread trauma.

A Pathway

The Substance Abuse and Mental Health Services Administration (SAMHSA, 2012) explains that trauma "results from an event, series of events, or set of circumstances that is experienced by an individual as physically or emotionally harmful or threatening and that has lasting adverse effects on the individual's functioning and physical, social, emotional, or spiritual well-being." We can experience "single incident trauma," like an assault, or "complex trauma," resulting from a series of incidents like chronic abuse or emotional neglect (Herman 2015).

At least two-thirds of adults have experienced some form of trauma, and a large CDC study indicates that the more we're exposed to adverse childhood experiences (ACEs) like divorce, sexual abuse, or substance abuse, the more likely we'll experience negative physical and mental health outcomes like heart disease, cancer, depression, and anxiety (Anda et al. 2006). Researchers also link physical neglect and emotional abuse with memory deficits and poorer cognitive performance in older adults (Majer et al. 2010).

We carry our own trauma histories, yet we may also experience secondary traumatic stress. As we bear witness to students' trauma stories, we may feel fear, exhaustion, guilt, cynicism, or avoidance, which can lead to emotional burnout (National Child Traumatic Stress Network 2011). However, acknowledging trauma's various forms doesn't mean that we're surrendering to it. Nadine Burke Harris says, "I don't think forgetting about adversity or blaming it is useful. The first step is taking its measure and looking clearly at the impact and risk as neither a tragedy nor a fairy tale but a meaningful reality in between." With self-awareness, we have greater power to navigate our own emotions and respond more effectively to others.

An Action

Take a few moments to complete the ACE quiz (see Additional Resources).

Guiding Questions

Consider how trauma might influence the way you respond to students and colleagues, and reflect on the following:

- Identify the positive relationships and supports you experienced throughout your life. How have they influenced your social and emotional development?

- How does your history influence the qualities you bring to your work in schools?

Benefits

Although educators tend to focus on *students'* needs as they develop trauma-sensitive practices, it's crucial to acknowledge our own vulnerabilities and draw on a repertoire of self-care tools. How we respond to stress in the short term can have long-term effects. Mindfulness practices lessen the effects of ACEs (Whitaker et al. 2014).

As we become more aware of the circumstances that trigger bodily distress and unpleasant emotions, we can develop personal coping skills and share them with one another. Recent research on teacher self-care points to the importance of community care and supportive relationships on our well-being—a we're-in-this-together approach (Luthar and Mendes 2020). As colleagues, we can create our *own* supportive spaces for our health and well-being.

Additional Resources

- "Take the ACE Quiz," Harvard University's Center on the Developing Child, https://developingchild.harvard.edu/media-coverage/take-the-ace-quiz-and-learn -what-it-does-and-doesnt-mean

- "Dimensions of Difference and Similarity Reflection," *Greater Good in Education,* https://ggie.berkeley.edu/practice/dimensions-of-difference-and-similarity -reflection

Week 42: Creating Safe Spaces

Have you ever experienced panic symptoms? I have: Terror floods me as I struggle to catch my breath; heat rises through my body. I'm dizzy, and my heart is pounding. There's a desperate desire to escape. The symptoms can hit out of the blue. You feel like your body is betraying you. It's such a helpless, out-of-control feeling.

I've also witnessed full-blown panic attacks—the desperation in a charged-up body, the alarm, and disorientation that can last for five to twenty minutes. Panic symptoms can be an expression of trauma (Bryant and Panasetis 2001). When I think about a colleague or child experiencing similar (or worse) symptoms at school, the first thing I want for them is a sense of safety.

A Pathway

Last week we reflected on the childhood events that can influence our mental and physical health. Now let's look at how past traumas can play out in the moment. As we engage with our students each day, any stimulus that reminds us of an overwhelming experience can trigger the original feelings or behaviors we developed to cope with that event. For example, unpredictability, a loss of control, an experience of rejection or confrontation; or feelings of vulnerability, shame, fear, or embarrassment may spark a range of responses, including tearfulness, paralyzed silence, rapid breathing, clenched fists, and tensed bodies. Trauma can violate our physical, social, and emotional safety. In those moments when our bodies feel threatened, we need the resources to feel safe again (Dorado et al. 2016).

As the adults in the room, teachers can offer students and ourselves physical and emotional spaces to regain a sense of calm and control. For example, we can structure learning experiences to ensure clear, predictable routines for students. Rather than catching them off guard with unclear goals and open-ended activities, we can provide rituals like daily classroom meetings, transitional cues between lessons with bells or music, and clear explanations of upcoming tasks. We tend to feel safer when we know what to expect (Dorado and Zakrzewski 2013).

However, in those charged-up moments when the amygdala—the emotion center of the brain—activates the body's stress system, some people dissociate and feel as if they're outside of their bodies, looking in. If you see a student suffering like this, there are ways

WEEK 42

to regain a sense of control. Label what is happening (to facilitate some psychological distance) and then offer the student options. Taking deep, slow breaths can slow the heart rate, but for some victims of trauma, focusing solely on the breath can be triggering, so offering different options is important: "You look frustrated or upset. Would you like to take a break and grab some water or spend a few minutes in the classroom library?" With a couple of reasonable options in play, we give students the agency to make a choice and do the next best thing for themselves in that moment (see Additional Resources).

An Action

This week, try an awareness practice that focuses purely on the senses called the 5-4-3-2-1 Sensory Grounding Technique. When you arrive in a new place that makes you slightly uncomfortable or when you experience a threat to your social, emotional, or even physical safety, redirect your attention to your senses by noting five things you see, four you touch, three you hear, two you smell, and one you taste.

Guiding Questions

After you've tried this practice several times on your own or with a group of colleagues or students, respond to the following:

- What did you notice in yourself as you moved through the practice? Describe your experience. If you shared this practice at school, did you debrief with practice participants? What did they say? What did you observe?

- When do you think you would try this practice again? Why?

Benefits

Sensory grounding practices are effective because they shift your focus away from the mental turmoil you're experiencing to focus on the here and now—your current reality. Painful experiences like traumatic flashbacks or panic symptoms demand the attention of our brains and bodies, yet sensory grounding can slowly pull us out of an emotional tailspin and into the present moment (Gard et al. 2011).

Over time, chronic stress or repeated trauma triggers can wear down our body's stress response system. However, we have tools at our fingertips to support ourselves and our students. And the good news is that our brains can and do change. Neuroplasticity—the brain's malleability—is essential to our survival, adaptation, resilience, and healing from the effects of toxic stress and trauma. So let's focus on our potential for growth and healing.

Additional Resources

- Bessel van der Kolk, *The Body Keeps the Score*

- "A 5-Step Mindfulness Grounding Technique to Ease Anxiety and Why Mindfulness Works," *Cognition Today,* https://cognitiontoday.com/5-step-mindfulness-grounding-technique-to-ease-anxiety-why-it-works

- "Making a Practice Trauma-Informed," *Greater Good in Education,* https://ggie.berkeley.edu/making-a-practice-trauma-informed

---

Week 43: Fostering a Sense of Belonging

Will I fit in? Can I succeed here? Will I be welcomed? Worries about belonging abound in schools. And these concerns are thrown into sharp relief for students and colleagues who are frequently marginalized. We've defined single-incident trauma and complex trauma, but "insidious trauma" occurs through ongoing experiences of marginalization and objectification based on racism, heterosexism, ageism, ableism, sexism, and other forms of oppression (Root 1992). Michael Schreiner describes insidious trauma as a "constant but barely perceptible tapping on your shoulder" rather than a "powerful punch to the face" (see Additional Resources). That incessant tapping may come in the form of daily insults, bullying behaviors, and subtle forms of exclusion—a shrug, a roll of the eyes, a turning away. Insidious trauma can chip away at someone's sense of self and make them question whether they belong.

A Pathway

The universal need to belong influences our capacity for learning and well-being (Baumeister and Leary 1995). Belonging is "an individual's experience of feeling that they are, or are likely to be, accepted and respected as a valued contributor in a specific environment" (Bailey and Stroman 2021, 3). As humans, we search our environments for cues that we're accepted and welcomed. We look to our daily interactions with others, we try to determine the unspoken rules in classrooms and schools, and we seek out examples of seemingly successful others who look like us and sound like us. Of course, our perceptions are shaped by our identities and past experiences of exclusion or inclusion (Bailey and Stroman 2021). Fortunately, a sense of belonging can develop over time (Walton and Brady 2021).

People from traditionally marginalized groups are more likely to experience worry about belonging because they regularly navigate stereotypes. In fact, researchers have studied the emotional burden of negative stereotypes on the academic performance of Black and female students (Steele 2010). "Stereotype threat" is that pressure someone feels when they worry that they'll somehow reinforce a negative stereotype, which can undermine their performance (Steele 1997). This additional worry can be distracting and provoke anxiety—sometimes leading students to disengage socially and academically (Walton and Cohen 2007). However, a large group of researchers have been adapting and testing a remarkably successful social-belonging intervention with racially diverse groups of students from middle school through college.

An Action

First, gather a few quotes, stories, or positive school climate survey results from a diverse group of students older than your current students. Use this information to (1) normalize the challenges and worries that students from all backgrounds experience when they're transitioning into a new classroom or school, and (2) to communicate the idea that a sense of belonging changes over time. If students realize that their fear about fitting in is normal and will change, they're less likely to let a handful of negative experiences discourage them.

These stories can come in many forms, but here are two examples (Goyer et al. 2019, 16, minor edits):

Middle school is scary at first but it gets better.... I worried I wouldn't find my classes and that I'd forget my locker combination. But teachers and staff care about you. Once I got lost, but the people I asked showed me the way. Even when I got in trouble or didn't do well in class the teachers showed me respect. They are easy to talk to, and they listen to what you have to say. I have good friends now.... I get along well with my teachers, and I feel at home here.

I didn't like taking tests at the beginning of sixth grade.... I thought I wasn't prepared and that my teachers and other people would think I wasn't smart. Sometimes when I had to take a test my stomach hurt. But the teachers were really nice. They helped me get better even if I didn't do well at first. Now I know I can trust people here.

After you share this information, ask students to write a brief persuasive letter that normalizes the transition into their school or classroom, and encourage future students to be hopeful about it. In this case, your students aren't simply passively receiving information; they have the power to reassure others that a sense of belonging can grow over time.

Guiding Questions

Now describe what happened.

- Did you share student quotes or stories (or positive school climate survey data) during class? Or ask a few students to speak to your class?

- How did students use that information to persuade others that a sense of belonging can grow over time?

- How did your students respond to this activity?

Benefits

Students who are confident that they belong engage more fully in learning. In fact, belonging is closely linked to health, well-being, achievement, and identity (Walton and Brady 2021). Studies with sixth graders link the intervention above with lower levels of stereotype threat, a reduction in disciplinary referrals and absences, higher levels of belonging, higher grades, and improved student attitudes across sixth grade (Borman et al. 2019; Goyer et al. 2019).

Of course, the problem of belonging at school is much bigger than one student-based intervention, and it's worth asking ourselves what we're asking them to "belong to" in the first place. One of the key barriers to equity in school is, in fact, a lack of trauma-informed practices (Simmons et al. 2018), and there are many ways we can help to create safer and more welcoming environments.

Additional Resources

- Resmaa Menakem, *My Grandmother's Hands: Racialized Trauma and the Pathway to Mending Our Hearts and Bodies*

- "Micro Aggression and Insidious Trauma," *Evolution Counseling,* https://evolutioncounseling.com/micro-aggression-and-insidious-trauma

---

Week 44: Encouraging Healing-Centered Practices

"That's so gay." "You speak English well." "What are you?" Microaggressions are every-day slights, insults, indignities, and put-downs—intentional or not—to people from marginalized groups (Sue 2010). Microaggressions can result in post-traumatic stress symptoms, anxiety, depression, and substance abuse—as well as lowered academic performance (Keels et al. 2017). Why? Because people who experience chronic microaggressions can internalize them—and those statements can gnaw away at their sense of control over outcomes in their lives (Lambert et al. 2009), so it's crucial to consider how we educators respond to our students' struggles.

We must be thoughtful about how we respond to unfamiliar or unanticipated student behaviors. A trauma-informed approach would avoid a self-protective threat-based response ("What is wrong with you?") and use a more thoughtful query ("What happened to you?"). However, according to researcher Shawn Ginwright (2018), a healing-centered response asks, "What is right? Do I really see my students' strengths? And do they?"

A Pathway

In his groundbreaking article, Ginwright (2018) encourages us to focus on "possibility," or well-being, instead of "pathology," or trauma. He proposes a focus on "healing-centered engagement" that addresses "the well-being we want, rather than the symptoms we want to suppress." Healing-centered engagement builds on trauma-informed approaches with an assets-based, collective view of healing. Rather than focusing on individual experiences of trauma, this holistic approach draws on community-based healing practices from across the globe, like restorative justice, mindfulness and nonviolent communication, prayer circles and other communal gatherings, and cultural practices like drumming, dance, or song, along with more contemporary urban practices like performance art or hip hop (Ginwright 2015). Healing-centered engagement "acknowledges that young people are much more than the worst thing that happened to them, and builds upon their experiences, knowledge, skills, and curiosity as positive traits to be enhanced" (Ginwright 2018).

With this rich, strengths-based approach to healing in mind, educators can play a role in flipping the deficit-based scripts that play out in classrooms. Here is one small but powerful way to shift your classroom culture. As an alternative to microaggressions, researcher Todd Pittinsky recommends microaffirmations—small actions that can make students feel welcome, valued, and encouraged (Pittinsky 2016)—such as nodding, making eye contact, referring to students by name, calling on all students equally, praising a wide range of actions, and using inclusive language, like "families" rather than "parents." He suggests that microaffirmations can be transformative—not only influencing students' academic work but also improving student well-being and fostering a positive school climate.

An Action

This week practice using at least one or two microaffirmations: using welcoming and inclusive language, positively reinforcing students through praise, or consciously acknowledging students by name during class discussions and activities.

Guiding Questions

- What do you observe in yourself and your students as you focus more on microaffirmations?

- What additional strength-based supports and practices could you incorporate?

- More broadly, how do you encourage healing-centered engagement among your students and colleagues?

Benefits

During a year-long study of over 1,200 teachers in fourteen states, researchers Pittinsky and Montoya (2016) found that student achievement increased when white teachers regularly encouraged and modeled welcoming and affirming behaviors among traditionally marginalized students of different races, ethnicities, genders, and abilities. Ginwright (2018) reminds us that a healing-centered response to trauma looks for "what is right" more than what is wrong. Students benefit when we shift our lens from the negative to the positive.

Most trauma research addresses how to support youth *after* a traumatic experience, but we can and should work proactively to disrupt and reduce some of these systemic sources of trauma before they affect our students. If we want to take a more holistic approach to addressing trauma, it's crucial for leaders and staff to review school policies with a trauma-sensitive lens. For example, does your school's discipline policy default to exclusionary practices (like suspensions or expulsions), or does it focus more on healing-centered, restorative practices? To what degree are you tracking, grouping, labeling or mislabeling students in ways that might limit their capacity for learning? Do all students have access to the material and human resources they need to learn and thrive? If not, what adjustments can be made? While tackling these questions, we can consciously focus on our students' well-being through strengths-based approaches to learning and a spirit of collective care (Wilson and Richardson 2020). Instead of simply *reacting* to pain and trauma, we can create conditions that foster joy and growth.

Additional Resources

- "Speak Up at School: How to Respond to Everyday Prejudice, Bias, and Stereotypes," *Learning for Justice,* https://www.learningforjustice.org/magazine/publications/speak-up-at-school

- "Making Classrooms and Schools Trauma-Informed and Healing-Centered," *Greater Good in Education,* https://ggie.berkeley.edu/trauma-trauma-informed-and-resiliency-informed-schools

Caring for Your Community

In a real sense all life is inter-related.... I can never be what I ought to be until you are what you ought to be.

—Martin Luther King Jr.

If you're looking for some fun "homework" revolving around this month's theme, watch the Emmy Award-winning television show *Ted Lasso*. American-turned-European football coach Ted Lasso can teach us a lot about building trust and what it means to be part of a community—even when we feel like we don't belong. His unfailing positivity and heartfelt, daily investment in every person in his AFC Richmond team carries him far beyond his meager knowledge of the game. It's all about relationships for Ted.

If we want to reform schools, we can follow his lead by honoring and appreciating all of the individuals who make up our team, too.

Week 45: Building Trust with Colleagues

All educators want meetings to be meaningful and productive, but that's not always what happens. There was a time in my career when I walked into meetings with pit-in-my-stomach dread. With a shift in leadership, I began to feel unappreciated (even useless), less empowered to do good work, and much less connected to my colleagues. The pervasive silence in that meeting room made me feel queasy. We teachers tended to leave those meetings, walk down the hall, and close our doors—and keep them closed. It was easier that way.

If we don't feel a sense of agency, belonging, and competence as educators (Deci and Ryan 2012), our morale and motivation suffer. And if our collegial relationships aren't strong, we're less likely to collaborate—and our students and schools suffer the consequences.

A Pathway

The core component necessary for quality relationships in school is trust, and we build "relational trust" as colleagues through our interactions in group settings (Bryk and Schneider 2003). Even in our day-to-day exchanges, we're assessing risks. *Should I reveal my thoughts? Does this person have good intentions? Can I be honest and vulnerable?* As we have more positive exchanges, our sense of trust can grow (Finnegan and Daly 2017).

If you want to foster trust among the adults in your school, incorporate positive interactions into your staff meetings—large and small. Oakland Unified School District leaders and the Collaborative for Academic, Social, and Emotional Learning (CASEL) designed a meeting framework that features three signature meeting practices that promote social and emotional well-being:

- Welcoming inclusion activities (<10 minutes)

- Engaging strategies (<15 minutes)

- Optimistic closures (<5 minutes)

A welcoming ritual or activity can draw on past experiences, include and connect everyone in the room, and establish a sense of safety and predictability. Engaging strategies can include brain breaks, individual think time, or active process strategies in pairs or small groups. The idea is to provide time for creating meaning and connecting with others. Finally, an optimistic closure can reinforce the topic of the day and encourage reflection and plans for moving forward positively. (See Additional Resources for sample activities.)

An Action

Volunteer to incorporate a welcoming ritual, an engaging strategy, or an optimistic closure in one of your upcoming meetings. If you're meeting remotely, ask everyone to share a picture on their phone that brings them joy. Invite your colleagues to engage in individual "think time" followed by a discussion of student work, and end optimistically by sharing an appreciation for someone in the room or finishing this sentence stem: "One thing that makes me hopeful this week is…"

Guiding Questions

Grab your journal and respond to one or more of the following questions:

- What are some of the most memorable staff meetings or group collaborations you've experienced? Why?

- What are your best ideas for welcoming, relationship-building activities to incorporate into staff meetings or gatherings?

- If you've already shared a new meeting ritual or activity, what did you choose? How did your colleagues respond?

- How do you know when there's a sense of relational trust among group members?

Benefits

Researchers Bryk and Schneider (2003) studied four hundred Chicago elementary schools across a decade and determined that "relational trust" among staff members was *the* key ingredient associated with an increase in student learning. Why? We need high levels of trust to collaborate effectively, learn together, process complex information, and take collective action. Recent studies confirm that staff trust and communication contribute to "odds-beating" school outcomes (Leis et al. 2017), and colleagues' and school leaders' ongoing expression of care and compassion can decrease burnout and increase job satisfaction and job commitment (Eldor and Shoshani 2016).

Based on observations of educators' daily interactions, researchers also discovered that respect, personal regard, job-role competence, and personal integrity all contributed to a sense of relational trust (Bryk and Schneider 2003). As we consciously create more authentic, inclusive opportunities for sharing, learning, and community building as adults, we *can* build trust so that everyone benefits—our students, most of all.

Additional Resources

- "SEL Three Signature Practices Playbook," CASEL, https://schoolguide.casel.org/uploads/2018/12/CASEL_SEL-3-Signature-Practices-Playbook-V3.pdf

- "Staff Meeting Rituals That Build Trust and Community," *Greater Good in Education,* https://ggie.berkeley.edu/practice/staff-meeting-rituals-that-build-trust-and-community

---

Week 46: Creating Stronger Relationships with Students

As a first-year high school teacher, I was overwhelmed by the number of students I met each day—over 160 ninth and tenth graders. How could I possibly connect with each one? Of course, I learned strategies for reaching out and building trust, like using the 2x10 strategy or dialogue journals, and I began incorporating more informal check-ins and conferences. I also focused on getting to know one small group of students each week (see Additional Resources).

However, a moment or two of connection in the middle of a busy day can feel like a drop in the bucket—especially when your students' struggles weigh heavily on you. You may be aware of students who are currently homeless, grieving the loss of a recently deported parent, or fearful and unsafe at home. And then there are those quiet, sullen students who share little…and you wonder.

A Pathway

Resilient children and teens often have at least one stable, caring, and committed adult in their lives. Research tells us that supportive relationships, adaptive skill-building, and positive experiences increase resilience, and as we tip the scale toward more positive rather than negative experiences each day, we grow in strength and adaptability (National Scientific Council on the Developing Child 2015).

Although toxic stress can reduce the size and number of neural connections in our brains, positive encounters can bolster neural connections and feed healthy brain development. Researcher Pamela Cantor and her colleagues (2019) explain that our experiences are "stressors" that can lead to brain growth, strengthening neural pathways and creating new ones. "If experiences are interpersonally rich, predictable, and patterned, and if stressful experiences are not overwhelming, the brain becomes more connected, integrated, and functionally capable over time, increasing its adaptivity and resilience to future stress" (Cantor et al. 2019, 311).

A rich array of educational research says that relationships drive healthy learning and development. We're also learning more about the characteristics of student-teacher relationships that feed positive development. These include things like emotional attunement, trust, consistency, and multiple opportunities to learn. In addition, teachers' responsiveness, high expectations, and belief in students' capabilities all feed students' self-concept and sense of themselves as learners (Osher et al. 2020).

If you're like me, this information may ramp up the pressure: *I must be a skilled instructional designer and facilitator of meaningful learning experiences—and an exceptionally caring and responsive teacher, too?!* The biggest mistake I made as a new teacher was assuming that I alone was responsible for meeting the needs of every student who walked into my classroom. We educators cannot do this work in isolation. At the same time, it doesn't happen by chance. Here is one way to make sure everyone in your school has at least one adult contact, cheerleader, and supporter.

An Action

Meet with a group of your colleagues (such as a disciplinary or grade-level team) to do some "relationship-mapping." List *all* the students in your classes and identify which of you have relationships with those students. Then pinpoint students who may benefit from additional care and support. (For a well-scaffolded, adaptable version of this practice, including a ready-made spreadsheet, see Additional Resources.)

Guiding Questions

After you review the document you've completed as a team, journal about what surprised you.

- Are there students who fall under the radar?

- What are your biggest questions and concerns about the students who need more support and care?

As you consider a plan for reaching out to these students, remind yourself of the teachers who motivated you. Journal about what they did.

- How did they relate to you?

- Why did they play a powerful role in your life?

- How might you draw from this experience to inform your current relationships?

Benefits

Positive student-teacher relationships contribute to student engagement, achievement, self-regulation, and social-emotional competence. Strong relationships can serve as a buffer for students who are struggling with challenges at home or at school (Osher et al. 2020). In fact, more researchers are studying the effects of teachers' "caring" behaviors. For example, a survey of middle school students found that the more students perceived teachers' care for them—in the form of conscientiousness, supportiveness, and inclusiveness—the less likely they were to display problem behaviors or to struggle with emotions or relationships with peers (Zhang et al. 2019). The challenges and traumas our students face are real, but we can support resilience and healing, turning "toxic" stress into "tolerable" stress (National Scientific Council on the Developing Child 2015).

Additional Resources

- "Relationship Mapping Strategy," *Making Caring Common,* https://mcc.gse.harvard.edu/resources-for-educators/relationship-mapping-strategy

- "Connecting with Students," *Greater Good in Education,* https://ggie.berkeley.edu/collection/connecting-with-students

---

Week 47: Connecting with Families

During my tenure as a teacher educator, the importance of parent-teacher relationships often fell to the bottom of my program's priority list: "By the way, make sure to communicate frequently and effectively with families. That's important, too. Here are a few tips."

You may have had a similar experience. Our students take center stage as we do our best to navigate some of the common barriers to communication with families, including lack of time, resources, and training in culturally responsive communication (Willemse et al. 2018). Of course, your school may actively prioritize family engagement while stumbling over your collective assumptions about the families themselves and how to authentically engage with them.

When researchers studied educational professionals' values, beliefs, and attitudes about families, two distinct forms emerged: (1) a *deficit perspective* characterized by blame, dismissiveness, or paternalism, and (2) a *culturally responsive perspective* characterized by respect, empathy, and an awareness of structural barriers to authentic family-school connection. In some cases, these two lenses overlapped. These findings highlight the potential contrast between educators' stated values and their "deficit-based" and "school-centric" assumptions (Lasater et al. 2021). No doubt this inconsistency can undermine trust and authentic relationship building.

A Pathway

Thankfully, we educators are beginning to adjust our lenses so that we see our institutions—and ourselves—more clearly while consciously engaging our own biases and assumptions. Research reflects a slow shift in educators' understanding of what it means to relate meaningfully to students' families: from "involvement" to "engagement" to "partnership." With *involvement,* "family support" primarily means event attendance and provision of supplies and resources. *Engagement* focuses more on the educator's role in welcoming families, learning more about them, and inviting ongoing participation at school. *Partnership,* however, features trust, meaningful relationships, co-construction of event goals and agendas, and a focus on the family's knowledge and strengths (Goodall and Montgomery 2014).

Karen Mapp and Paul Kuttner (2013) have studied family-school partnership strategies and developed a systems-level "Dual Capacity-Building Framework," representing what this ongoing reciprocity of relationship can look like. "The Framework reveals that, in order for family-school partnerships to succeed, the adults responsible for children's education must learn and grow, just as they support learning and growth among students" (Mapp and Kuttner 2013, 25).

We can't learn and grow as adults without a sense of humility and an understanding that we have a lot to learn from the families in our communities. We can invite more equitable family engagement by honoring families' languages and preferred methods of communication, providing regular listening sessions that include community liaisons as interpreters or facilitators, and offering home visits (Jacques and Villegas 2018). Family-school interventions that have the most positive influence on students' social and emotional health draw on relationship-building processes like collaborating around students' academic or behavioral goals with family participation informed by their values and strengths (Sheridan et al. 2019).

An Action

Each day this week, select a student and send a strengths-based, positive message to their family, congratulating the student on an accomplishment or action. Over time, you can track and celebrate each of your students' strengths, talents, and successes with their caregivers.

Guiding Questions

However, before you reach out to students' families this week, take a few minutes to reflect on how past experiences influence your beliefs about families and their participation in their children's education.

- How was your family involved in your day-to-day schooling when you were young?

- As an educator, consider recent experiences with parents or families. Have they been negative, neutral, positive?

- How does your school currently communicate beliefs about the role of families in student learning? How does that influence your work?

Benefits

If we want to foster honest, authentic, and respectful relationships with families, it's crucial to explore our sociocultural backgrounds, childhood experiences, and professional experiences, as well as our school or district norms around family engagement (Souto-Manning and Swick 2006)—all of which influence our beliefs.

When we engage and *partner* with our students' families, rather than simply seeing them as "helpers," we develop a sense of shared ownership of outcomes (Goodall and Montgomery 2014). Further, a review of 117 studies indicates that when schools invite families to partner with them in their children's learning, students' social and emotional learning and well-being improves along with their grades (Sheridan et al. 2019).

As we appreciate our students' and families' knowledge, strengths, and contributions, we become better partners. As one school leader explains, "Every parent wants to know that you care about their child. Honestly, that's the bottom line to literally everything that we do…it is a beautiful thing. The more diverse, the better. It challenges you, but it also opens your eyes to amazing things in the world, and how we don't all do things the same, but at the end of the day we all love our families. We all want the best for our kids" (Lasater et al. 2021, 15).

Additional Resources

- "The Dual Capacity-Building Framework for Family-School Partnerships," *Dual Capacity,* https://www.dualcapacity.org

- "Strategies for Equitable Family Engagement," *State Support Network,* https://oese.ed.gov/files/2020/10/equitable_family_engag_508.pdf

---

Week 48: Engaging with Your Community

My daughter will never forget her "Change the World" project. When I ask her why, she simply responds, "Because we got out and *did* something."

Her eighth-grade social studies teacher tasked the class with choosing a social issue, researching the problem and its possible solutions, and planning some form of advocacy or action. I don't think I've ever seen her more energized, confident, and engaged in a school project. And now, years later, I still run into current students from her old school canvasing our neighborhood, advocating for policies that protect refugees, homeless youth, or animals used for product testing.

Most of the time, "learning" takes place within classrooms—driven by academic standards that sometimes feel disconnected from real-world issues and challenges. Even when we venture outside to learn, we tend to consider how community engagement will benefit *us*. We can also be ill-equipped to critically examine, understand, and partner meaningfully with neighborhood stakeholders on community issues (Green 2017). Yet rich opportunities for authentic learning and relationship building exist right outside our doors, where we can grow in knowledge about the world while fostering the skills needed to participate in changing it.

A Pathway

Teachers and students at multiple grade levels engage in project-based learning in response to community needs. For example, teachers in Chicago supported students in identifying real-world environmental concerns like the pollution in a nearby river. Interdisciplinary teams in math, science, language arts, and civics scaffolded students' learning as they explored the larger question: "What systems are we in, and how do we affect those systems?" Students learned about pollution and ecosystems; developed a conservancy plan; collected and analyzed water-testing and trash survey data; shared their findings in plays, presentations, and on their own website; and made a plan for restoring a riverbank with a community partner (Bouillon and Gomez 2001).

Universities are also spearheading partnerships with local community organizations. My long-held skepticism about "ivory tower" academics fell away during my tenure at Seattle University. Its Center for Community Engagement serves as a hub in the middle of the city—fostering long-term partnerships with 132 community organizations focused on health care, housing, environmental sustainability, foster care, and more.

The Center focuses on social change, engaging students and faculty in service learning, community-based research, and ongoing community engagement.

Much like school-family partnerships, authentic school-community partnerships require self-awareness and organizational awareness. We can't sustain a meaningful relationship without really understanding each other—and the power dynamics at play. Green (2017) explains that a "community-based equity audit" includes interrupting any "deficit" views we have about the community, engaging in active "inquiry" and shared experiences in community, establishing a balanced leadership team, and collecting strengths-based community data that leads to action. In other words, if we can proceed with humility, acknowledging any assumptions we may hold while fostering an open-minded approach to learning from and with the community, we can authentically collaborate on a plan to share resources and respond to real-world community needs. This takes time, but as we connect with organizations in our communities, we create opportunities for our students and colleagues to experience deeper and more meaningful learning.

An Action

Jump on the web, pick up the phone, or take a field trip to explore at least one community-based organization in your neighborhood—a nonprofit, an after-school program, or a faith-based organization. As you learn more about the organization's mission and the resources it provides, consider how you might nurture a partnership with them in the future.

Guiding Questions

Pull out your journal and map out the possibilities.

- Which organization interests you? Why?

- How might you foster a relationship with them? What kinds of resource sharing and collaboration do you envision? How might you support this organization's mission?

- Can you picture a project that could support this organization and provide a valuable service-learning experience for your students?

Benefits

When new teachers participate in cultural-immersion activities as part of their professional preparation, they shift misperceptions about the people in their community and build meaningful relationships with students that can positively influence their academic achievement (Cooper 2007). Further, students who engage in civic behaviors report greater well-being when they are helping others or caring for the environment by recycling or conserving resources (Wray-Lake et al. 2019).

As students learn to contribute to their communities, they also practice thinking beyond themselves, which may ultimately help them to be more positive, empowered, and purposeful. And as we learn in context—seeing ourselves as part of a collective—we also grow a stronger sense of belonging and connection to our community.

Additional Resources

- "Successful School-Based Partnerships: What Does It Take?," *William Penn Foundation,* https://williampennfoundation.org/what-we-are-learning/successful-school-based-partnerships-what-does-it-take

- "Resources for Building Community Partnerships," *Edutopia,* https://www.edutopia.org/article/community-business-partnerships-resources

---

Looking Ahead and Sustaining Hope

Be as you wish to seem.

—Socrates

At a time when teacher burnout is unprecedented and many things are out of our control, I regularly take solace in these words from the Serenity Prayer: "Grant me the serenity to accept the things I cannot change, the courage to change the things I can, and the wisdom to know the difference." Then I pool my energies to act on behalf of the good each day.

At this point in our journey, we've explored forty-eight evidence-based actions we can take on behalf of ourselves and our students. We've learned more about our emotions and thoughts, and how to be in the moment, savor good things, celebrate creativity, reach out, and sustain our relationships. In this last chapter, we will explore how to move forward with confidence, motivation, courage, and hope.

Week 49: Believing in Yourself

When I sat down for a coaching session with an anxious new teacher, she described cycles of nervousness and self-consciousness while she was teaching. "It's not about what I'm doing; this is *in me*," she explained. "My colleague says that she can sense my lack of confidence." As she described her childhood and her intense training as a musician, she pinpointed her ingrained need for perfection. Classrooms full of humans are never perfect. And that's *okay*. Over time, this teacher learned to let go of her desire for perfection and cut herself some slack.

Of course, teachers contending with workload and classroom stress can also experience lower self-efficacy—the belief in your capacity to handle the tasks and challenges of your job (Klassen and Chiu 2010). And even if you have been in the profession for a while, your confidence can suffer. Daily stressors can pile up, leading to emotional exhaustion, a sense of detachment from your work, and the feeling that you simply aren't as capable as you thought you were. These are the three characteristics of burnout (Maslach and Leiter 2016).

Bottom line: whether you're new to the profession or have been in the game for years, your belief in yourself as an educator plays a fundamental role in your day-to-day motivation and job satisfaction (Barni et al. 2019; Klassen and Chiu 2010).

A Pathway

As an educator, you may know the things that can enhance your students' sense of self-efficacy: personal successes, vicarious experiences like watching others thrive and grow, and social persuasion—feedback and encouragement from others that motivates them to keep trying (see Additional Resources). We adults also benefit when we celebrate our personal accomplishments, learn from each other, and receive honest, supportive feedback from our colleagues. In fact, researchers studying new teachers' experiences during their internships discovered that their relationships with their mentor teachers played a critical role—influencing both their stress and self-efficacy levels (Klassen and Durksen 2014).

Tracking your own successes and learning from others' modeling and feedback can help you to gain (or regain) confidence, but it's also important to learn how to navigate your internal experience: your thoughts, emotions, and beliefs about your work. We've focused on navigating our inner worlds throughout this book—learning how to question thoughts and beliefs, observe and accept our experiences through mindfulness, and extend ourselves some kindness in challenging moments. Although teacher education primarily centers around instructional knowledge and skills, learning how to navigate self-criticism, soothe yourself, and redirect your thoughts and feelings may be even more critical to self-efficacy and job performance.

An Action

The next time you feel criticized or worried about your work performance, draw on one or more of the following self-affirmations to clarify your values and reframe your thinking (Morgan and Atkin 2016):

- What do I value in myself?

- What do I "stand for"?

- What is important to me?

- What are some of my successes and accomplishments?

Guiding Questions

Which of the prompts above are most effective in shifting your thoughts and emotions? Why?

Now, sit down with your journal and identify at least three things you generally do quite well. (If you're a classroom teacher, consider these three domains of educator self-efficacy: instructional strategies, classroom management, and student engagement.)

- How do these three skills or capacities align with your values?

- How might these skills or capacities influence your students' or colleagues' personal and professional growth?

- How can you draw on these skills or capacities in the coming week?

Benefits

Hours after drafting our action for this week, I realized how much I needed it. I participated in a panel discussion about burnout and well-being, and afterward, I found myself running through everything I said and how I said it—faulting myself for stumbling over my words and neglecting to share what I thought would be most helpful. (Ha!) Then I remembered this week's action, and drawing on the questions above, I discovered how "in the weeds" I was. The performance minutiae receded when I began to reconnect with what is important to me—and how I uphold my values. What a relief. This activity helped me to detach a little as I held on to my big-picture vision of supporting educators with love, compassion, and hope.

When researchers measured teachers' responses to prompts like these, they found that teachers' anxiety immediately decreased, and they experienced more positive emotions over time when compared to a control group (Morgan and Atkin 2016). I'm not surprised. Teachers' personal values drive their goals and behaviors at school while supporting their well-being and a sense of self-efficacy at work (Barni et al. 2019). In fact, teachers with stronger self-efficacy tend to report a zest for their work and a sense of academic optimism and hope (Sezgin and Erdogan 2015). As we learn to navigate our inner worlds and clarify what really matters in our work, we can also support each other by revisiting our collective goals and values, reflecting on our learning, and growing in confidence together.

Additional Resources

- "Strategies for Developing and Maintaining Self-Efficacy in Teachers," *The Education Hub,* https://theeducationhub.org.nz/strategies-for-developing-and -maintaining-self-efficacy-in-teachers

- "Three Ways Administrators Can Foster Teachers' Growth," *Greater Good,* https://greatergood.berkeley.edu/article/item/3_ways_administrators_can_foster _teachers_growth

---

Week 50: Finding Inspiration

I'm a little weary of the teacher-as-hero metaphor. I resist watching films about larger-than-life, inspiring teachers. Maybe that strikes you as strange, considering my positive focus throughout this book. I may resist this metaphor because I feel protective of my people. We put a lot of pressure on ourselves in the first place, and there are plenty of days when we don't live up to our self-imposed expectations—much less the image of the teacher-as-savior. Regardless, teachers undeniably play a lead role in their students' lives, so where do we find the zest and energy for our work when inspiration is waning?

Last week we explored how belief in our abilities develops as we experience successes and learn to affirm ourselves. However, self-efficacy also flourishes as we witness others' growth through "vicarious experience." In other words, we teachers also benefit from observing models.

A Pathway

In fact, self-efficacy and motivation go hand in hand. A belief in yourself can move you to action. And there are many other factors that energize us. A review of 130 teacher motivation studies indicates that personal characteristics—our interests, values, expectations, and prior experiences, as well as our working environment and relationships with colleagues and students, administrative support, and opportunities for learning—all affect our stress level, sense of autonomy, and our drive (Han and Yin 2016).

When your intrinsic motivation is waning, you can also draw inspiration from others—near or far, real or fictional. According to research, the individuals we admire represent some aspect of our ideal selves as they demonstrate moral courage through difficult times—and a desire to do good in the world. They can also inspire us to live more meaningful lives (Van Tongeren et al. 2018).

I recently asked colleagues to describe their personal heroes, and they primarily identified people in their immediate circle: family members, colleagues, and mentors. Their heroes were "nurturing," "kindhearted," "resilient," "a force to be reckoned with," and "loved learning for learning's sake." On days when you feel anything but heroic—whatever that means to you—you can summon up images of people you respect.

An Action

This week consider at least three of your personal heroes (real or fictional). If possible, print images of them, and post them in your classroom or office as reminders.

Guiding Questions

Grab your journal.

- Who inspires you? Why?

- Describe each person briefly. Consider the characteristics you share with them—or aspire to emulate. If each of these heroes were to identify a central goal or motivation in life, what would it be?

- How does this exercise help you to clarify what motivates you?

Benefits

Studies suggest that seeing images of heroes may inspire us to sense greater meaning in our lives—and even increase our drive to help others (Van Tongeren et al. 2018). And our enthusiasm for our work can influence our students' engagement and academic performance (Mahler et al. 2018).

After reviewing research about heroes, I see why idealized, based-on-a-true-story teacher movies irritate me. Apparently, *fictional* heroes can be more motivating because we're less likely to measure ourselves against an abstract symbol and find ourselves wanting. They're less psychologically threatening and allow us to protect our self-esteem (Van Tongeren et al. 2018).

Of course, it's also worth exploring how we define "hero" in the first place. My heroes are quietly courageous humans; they are real and vulnerable and authentic. My witty and wise aunt lives a simple life focused on *being* rather than performing. She makes me feel seen. My favorite co-teacher always invited me into her office, laid out an array of tea options, and then quietly prepared a cup for each of us, no matter how busy we were. This ritual—a calming act of attention and care—captures the person she is—and the kind of teacher I aspire to be.

Additional Resources

- Sam Intrator and Megan Scribner (eds.), *Teaching with Fire: Poetry That Sustains the Courage to Teach*

- "Twenty Inspiring Reasons Why You Love to Teach," *Edutopia,* https://www .edutopia.org/discussion/20-inspiring-reasons-why-you-love-teach

Week 51: Seeing Mistakes as Opportunities

Early in my teaching career, I had several recurring dreams. In one, the boys in my class walked around talking while many of the girls sat at their desks applying makeup and blow-drying their hair. In another, my classroom was so large and full that I needed a microphone, but I couldn't find one. In both, there was chaos. And no one could hear me. Now that I'm older and have a couple of graduate degrees under my belt, I still have a dream that I must return to high school (or college) to finish my last year due to a years-old transcript error. What niggling fears we educator-humans can carry in our performance-based, perfectionist culture—whether we're awake or asleep.

When researcher Patricia Phelps (2000) asked seventy-nine pre-service teachers about the mistakes they believed they would make in the classroom, they predicted at least forty-three different mistakes that fell into two categories: instructional and inter-personal. They described instructional concerns like not preparing enough or boring their students, as well as interpersonal fears that they wouldn't be firm enough or that they would get too close to their students.

When fear of failure affects self-worth, many will do everything in their power to avoid it. If you walk into your classroom fearing mistakes, you may take fewer risks. But Phelps's findings suggest that mistakes are actually "vehicles for educating" teachers, and that we can do a better job of realistically portraying teacher learning by creating professional environments where we openly share and reflect on our struggles.

A Pathway

I recently spotted an anonymous quote on Instagram that grabbed me: "Failure is just research unless you never try again." What if we truly viewed failure as research? Our beliefs play a powerful role in helping us navigate day-to-day stressors. If we think we have the resources to creatively implement a new curriculum, for example, we're more likely to view it as a *challenge* rather than a threat to our well-being—and we'll cope better with any resulting stress (Lazarus and Folkman 1984).

One resource teachers have at their fingertips is their love of learning, but that can be shadowed by fear of failure. Carol Dweck (2014) explains that our beliefs or mindsets about intelligence range from "fixed" (intelligence is static) to "growth" (intelligence is malleable). And our beliefs can influence our approach to learning—and our achievement.

If we want our students to see their mistakes as opportunities for learning, how can we emanate that mindset? Dweck (2014) suggests that teachers themselves can benefit from a growth mindset, reasonable goals, patience, and ongoing reflection: "A new teacher's mindset may have more to do with her success than her natural teaching talent. When she feels overwhelmed, her mindset will determine whether she gives up or sticks with it" (10).

Persistence can be learned. As teachers, we have a lot of power to influence our students' efforts by sharing our own vulnerability and identifying our own self-conscious emotions, our stops and starts during problem solving, and our commitment to keep going. One study demonstrates that when adults model persistence in working toward a goal, infants as young as fifteen months tend to mimic that behavior (Leonard et al. 2017). Further, when teachers see their own mistakes as learning tools, their persistence can evolve into a more positive, authentic investment in their professional development—they read more about teaching techniques and ideas, observe other teachers in action, and ask for feedback on their teaching from supervisors or colleagues they respect (Dweck 2014).

An Action

This week identify something you're struggling with right now. You may want to explore new ways to teach photosynthesis, or you might be resisting a difficult conversation with a co-teacher or student. Commit to seeing this stressor as a challenge—an opportunity for growth—rather than a threat to your well-being. Consider sharing this struggle with at least one trusted friend, mentor, or colleague (formally or informally).

Next, identify one new thing you'll try in addressing this challenge. Maybe you'll draw on an active listening strategy for the tough conversation, or you'll join an online educator community focused on innovative ways to teach science.

Guiding Questions

Describe in your journal the challenge and the new thing you tried.

- What did you observe? Did seeing what you were struggling with as a *challenge* shift your approach to it?

- Did experimenting with a new strategy or source of information help?

Benefits

When researchers reviewed thirty-eight studies of resilience in response to failure, errors, or mistakes, they found that more resilient individuals had lower levels of perfectionism and a more positive way of explaining past events: "My students didn't understand my lesson on quadratic equations today, but I'll try another approach tomorrow" (Johnson et al. 2017). And research also suggests that teachers' growth mindsets can be linked to the development of students' growth mindsets—particularly in boys (Mesler et al. 2021).

No doubt students feel more welcome to explore and authentically learn when they see their teachers unashamedly tackling day-to-day challenges and modeling persistence. One new teacher put it well: "I can see myself expecting perfection from myself rather than allowing humanness. This is a mistake because it would keep me from being 'real' to my students and I could very well get into a mindset of expecting perfection from them as well" (Phelps 2000, 45). Rather than fearing looming "failures," addressing our daily missteps head-on and seeing them as opportunities for learning frees all of us to appreciate learning for what it is—a process rather than a performance.

Additional Resources

- Carol Dweck, *Mindset: The New Psychology of Success*

- "Why We Should Embrace Mistakes in School," *Greater Good,* https://greatergood.berkeley.edu/article/item/why_we_should_embrace_mistakes_in_school

---

Week 52: Moving Forward with Hope

Hope is the thing with feathers that perches in the soul.

—Emily Dickinson

As a lover of poetry, I look to aspirational quotes for the magic they can provide. And thanks to great writers like Dickinson, I've nurtured a romanticized view of hope most of my life.

For me, hope appears as a moment of spiritual resonance when I just can't help feeling purposeful. It emerges, settles on my figurative shoulder, and gently guides me. Problem is—these poignant moments of clarity aren't always accessible to me. Instead of a lightness dwelling in my soul, I often feel forsaken, weighed down, and dark.

As much as I love hope as a pure feeling, it comes and goes. It's also not something that magically reveals itself out of the vastness of the sky to save me. I urge it into being. In fact, hope grows out of pragmatism, commitment, and *action*.

A Pathway

This book's introduction focused on hope. Based on Charles Snyder's (2002) classic theory, hope includes two forms of thinking. First, if you picture a way forward (along with alternative routes), you're practicing *pathway thinking*. Second, if you believe that you have the capacity to meet your valued goals through motivation and persistence, you're engaging in *agency thinking*. Based on this idea, each week in *Surviving Teacher Burnout* has featured a *pathway* and an *action*.

If these are the building blocks of hope, we might consider the secret sauce that enriches them to be our values. Research points to the undeniable links between goals, hope, and meaning in life (Feldman et al. 2018). And our values play a powerful role in guiding our intentions—especially long-term rather than short-term actions (Eyal et al. 2009). For example, I value human connection and want to build trusting relationships with my colleagues. However, if my focus is on short-term, day-to-day stressors like unanticipated meetings or mounting paperwork, the resulting exhaustion can prevent me from reaching out. But if I keep my head up and focus on the long-term benefits of healthy, emotionally sustaining relationships, I'm more likely to move forward with a plan for nurturing those relationships. Research suggests that we're more likely to act on value-based intentions when we connect them to a more distant future (Eyal et al. 2009).

To foster hope, have a long-term goal based on a valued "why" that gives you meaning, map out several ways to get there, and believe that you can.

An Action

As we come to the end of this book, I invite you to identify one long-term goal (for the upcoming season, the next six months, or even the next academic year) aligned with a value or values you hold. Outline three concrete steps you'll take to meet your goal. For each step, identify a possible obstacle and a way around it. Then take twenty minutes to visualize, as vividly as possible, how you'll meet this goal. As you imagine meeting this goal, draw on all your senses and picture what it would feel like to experience this outcome you desire for your life.

Guiding Questions

Reflect in your journal.

- How does this journey align with a value you hold?

- Do you have a mentor or supporter who might help you move toward that goal and navigate the obstacles?

- What do you feel when you envision meeting your goal?

Benefits

People who participated in an activity like this reported increases in hope, purpose, and career calling (compared to a control group); and one month later, they reported greater practical progress toward their goal (Feldman and Dreher 2012). Additional research with teachers suggests that hope influences the actions teachers take to enact a vision (Daoud and Parsons 2021). If we can see a pathway forward and believe in our ability to navigate it, we're more hopeful.

As educators, we can channel this form of hope into our work with students and colleagues, and hope can positively influence academic outcomes. Studies tell us that student hope can even mediate the relationship between socioeconomic status and grade point average (Dixson et al. 2018). When students experience hope through agency and pathway thinking, they're more likely to perceive obstacles and stressors as *challenges* rather than *threats.*

Yes, hope can be savored and experienced as a beautiful feeling full of possibility, but it also drives us forward as we enact our values and goals. And hope doesn't have to perch quietly in each of our souls—we can share it and live it, collectively. As an African proverb says, "If you want to go fast, go alone. If you want to go far, go together."

Additional Resources

- "How Hope Can Keep You Happier and Healthier," *Greater Good,* https://greatergood.berkeley.edu/article/item/how_hope_can_keep_you_happier_and_healthier

- "How to Help Students Believe in Themselves," *Greater Good,* https://greatergood.berkeley.edu/article/item/how_to_help_students_believe_in_themselves

Acknowledgments

Deep gratitude to the amazing humans who contributed to this book—whether directly or indirectly.

To my colleagues at the Greater Good Science Center—our mission informs so much of *Surviving Teacher Burnout*—its tone, structure, and research grounding emerge from my time with all of you. Vicki Zakrzewski, you brought me to the Center, and our work translating research into courses, articles, and online resources has been foundational to my evolving understanding of educator well-being. Mariah Flynn, your wide-ranging expertise and pragmatism ground me. Jason Marsh, I am so grateful for your kindness, leadership, and ongoing support. And to Kira Newman and Jeremy Smith, your expert editorial feedback at *Greater Good* magazine prepared me for this new adventure! Thank you.

Of course, there is also a larger community of scholars, researchers, and practitioners who enlighten and encourage me in sharing hopeful news with educators, including Elena Aguilar, Patricia Broderick, Shawn Ginwright, Daniel Goleman, Rick Hanson, Tish Jennings, Todd Kashdan, Dacher Keltner, Rhonda Magee, Parker Palmer, Kristin Neff, Rob Roeser, Kim Schonert-Reichl, Dan Siegel, Martin Seligman, Meena Srinivasan…and many more.

And there would be no book without New Harbinger's editors, who facilitated a smooth, positive writing process. Wendy Millstone, you saw the potential for this book and expertly guided me along the way. Jennifer Holder, you helped me to package my ideas more clearly. And Jennifer Eastman, I am so grateful for your masterful editing and careful eyes.

Finally, to my family (Dad, Mom, Richard, Ginger, Alex, and Isaac)—your support and encouragement mean the world to me. Meg, thank you for seeing and honoring my creative soul. And to Tim, my person—I am forever grateful for your steady, loving presence on this journey.

References

Aknin, L. B. et al. 2011. "Investing in Others: Prosocial Spending for (Pro)social Change." In *Positive Psychology as a Mechanism for Social Change,* edited by R. Biswas-Diener. London: Springer.

Aknin, L. B. et al. 2013. "Making a Difference Matters: Impact Unlocks the Emotional Benefits of Prosocial Spending." *Journal of Economic Behavior and Organization* 88: 90–95.

Allen, B. A. et al. 2019. "Outcomes of Meaningful Work." *Journal of Management Studies* 56 (3): 500–28.

Allen, S. 2018a. *The Science of Awe.* Greater Good Science Center. John Templeton Foundation. https://ggsc.berkeley.edu/images/uploads/GGSC-JTF_White_Paper-Awe_FINAL.pdf.

———. 2018b. *The Science of Generosity.* Greater Good Science Center. John Templeton Foundation. https://ggsc.berkeley.edu/images/uploads/GGSC-JTF_White_Paper-Generosity-FINAL.pdf.

Anda, R. F. et al. 2006. "The Enduring Effects of Abuse and Related Adverse Experiences in Childhood." *European Archives of Psychiatry and Clinical Neuroscience* 256 (3): 174–86.

Arendt, J. F. W. et al. 2019. "Mindfulness and Leadership: Communication as a Behavioral Correlate of Leader Mindfulness and Its Effect on Follower Satisfaction." *Frontiers in Psychology* 10: 667.

Arthur, J. et al. 2015. "The Good Teacher: Understanding Virtues in Practice." Birmingham, UK: Jubilee Centre for Character.

Ashar, Y. K. et al. 2017. "Empathic Care and Distress." *Neuron* 94 (6): 1263–73.

Aspinall, P. et al. 2015. "The Urban Brain: Analysing Outdoor Physical Activity with Mobile EEG." *British Journal of Sports Medicine* 49 (4): 272–76.

Avanzi, L. et al. 2018. "How to Mobilize Social Support Against Workload and Burnout." *Teaching and Teacher Education* 69: 154–67.

Baer, R. 2015. "Ethics, Values, Virtues, and Character Strengths in Mindfulness-Based Interventions." *Mindfulness* 6 (4): 956–69.

Bailey, K., and C. Stroman. 2021. *Structures for Belonging: A Synthesis of Research on Belonging-Supportive Learning Environments.* Student Experience Research Network. https://studentexperiencenetwork.org/wp-content/uploads/2021/03/Structures-for-Belonging-Executive-Summary.pdf.

Baker, K. C., and N. Mazza. 2004. "The Healing Power of Writing." *Journal of Poetry Therapy* 17 (3): 141–54.

Banicki, K. 2014. "Positive Psychology on Character Strengths and Virtues." *New Ideas in Psychology* 33: 21–34.

Barni, D., F. Danioni, and P. Benevene. 2019. "Teachers' Self-Efficacy: The Role of Personal Values and Motivations for Teaching." *Frontiers in Psychology* 10: 1645.

Barrett, L. F. 2006. Valence Is a Basic Building Block of Emotional Life." *Journal of Research in Personality* 40 (1): 33–55.

Bartz, J. A., J. Zaki, N. Bolger, and K. N. Ochsner. 2011. "Social Effects of Oxytocin in Humans." *Trends in Cognitive Sciences* 15 (7): 301–9.

Batson, C. D., N. Ahmad, D. A. Lishner, and J. A. Tsang. 2005. "Empathy and Altruism." In *Handbook of Positive Psychology,* edited by C. R. Snyder and S. J. Lopez. Oxford: Oxford University Press.

Batson, C. D., S. Early, and G. Salvarani. 1997. "Imagining How Another Feels Versus Managing How You Would Feel." *Personality and Social Psychology Bulletin* 23 (7): 751–58.

Baumeister, R. F., and M. Leary. 1995. "The Need to Belong: Desire for Interpersonal Attachments as a Fundamental Human Motivation." *Psychological Bulletin* 117: 497–529.

Beaumont, E., M. Durkin, C. J. H. Martin, and J. Carson. 2016. "Measuring Relationships Between Self-Compassion, Compassion Fatigue, Burnout, and Well-Being in Student Counsellors and Student Cognitive Behavioral Psychotherapists." *Counseling Psychotherapy Research Journal* 16: 15–23.

Beck, A. 1996. "Beyond Belief: A Theory of Modes, Personality, and Psychopathology." In *Frontiers of Cognitive Therapy,* edited by P. M. Salkovskis. New York: Guilford Press.

Berman, M. G., J. Jonides, and S. Kaplan. 2008. "The Cognitive Benefits of Interacting with Nature." *Psychological Science* 19 (12): 1207–12.

Bernhardt, B. C., and T. Singer. 2012. "The Neural Basis of Empathy." *Annual Review of Neuroscience* 35: 1–23.

Blatt, E., and P. Patrick. 2014. "An Exploration of Pre-Service Teachers' Experiences in Outdoor 'Places' and Intentions for Teaching in the Outdoors." *International Journal of Science Education* 36 (13): 2243–64.

Böhm, R., H. Rusch, and J. Baron. 2020. "The Psychology of Intergroup Conflict." *Journal of Economic Behavior & Organization* 178: 947–62.

Bono, G., S. Mangan, M. Fauteux, and J. Sender. 2020. "A New Approach to Gratitude Interventions in High Schools that Supports Student Wellbeing." *The Journal of Positive Psychology* 15 (5): 657–65.

Borman, G. D. et al. 2019. "Reappraising Academic and Social Adversity Improves Middle School Students' Academic Achievement, Behavior, and Well-Being." *Proceedings of the National Academy of Sciences of the United States of America* 116 (33): 16286–91.

Bouillon, L. M., and L. M. Gomez. 2001. "Connecting School and Community with Science Learning: Real-World Problems and School/Community Partnerships as Contextual Scaffolds." *Journal of Research in Science Teaching* 38 (8): 878–98.

Bowen, D. H., and B. Kisida. 2020. "Investigating Causal Effects of Arts Education Experiences." *Research Report for the Houston Independent School District* 7 (4): 1–28.

Brackett, M. A. et al. 2010. "Emotion-Regulation Ability, Burnout, and Job Satisfaction Among British Secondary-School Teachers." *Psychology in the Schools* 47 (4): 406–17.

Branwhite, T. 1988. "The Pass Survey: School-Based Preferences of 500+ Adolescent Consumers." *Educational Studies* 14 (2): 165–76.

Bratman, G. N. et al. 2015a. "The Benefits of Nature Experience: Improved Affect and Cognition." *Landscape and Urban Planning* 138: 41–50.

Bratman, G. N. et al. 2015b. "Nature Reduces Rumination and Subgenual Prefrontal Cortex Activation." *Proceedings of the National Academy of Sciences* 112 (28): 85–72.

Braun, S. S. et al. 2020. "Impacts of a Mindfulness-Based Program on Teachers' Forgiveness." *Mindfulness* 11: 1978–92.

Braun, T. D., C. L. Park, and A. Gorin. 2016. "Self-Compassion, Body Image, and Disordered Eating." *Body Image* 17: 117–31.

Breines, J. G., and S. Chen. 2012. "Self-Compassion Increases Self-Improvement Motivation." *Personality and Social Psychology Bulletin* 38 (9): 1133–43.

Bronk, K. C. et al. 2019. "Fostering Purpose Among Adolescents." *Journal of Character Education* 15 (2): 21–38.

Brown, E. L., C. K. Vesely, and L. Dallman. 2016. "Unpacking Biases: Developing Cultural Humility in Early Childhood and Elementary Teacher Candidates." *Teacher Educators Journal* 9: 75–96.

Bruehlman-Senecal, E., and O. Ayduk. 2015. "This Too Shall Pass: Temporal Distance and the Regulation of Emotional Distress." *Journal of Personality and Social Psychology* 108 (2): 356–75.

Bruneau, E. G., and R. Saxe. 2012. "The Power of Being Heard: The Benefits of 'Perspective-Giving' in the Context of Intergroup Conflict." *Journal of Experimental Social Psychology,* 48: 855–66.

Brunzell, T., H. Stokes, and L. Waters. 2018. "Why Do You Work with Struggling Students? Teacher Perceptions of Meaningful Work in Trauma-Impacted Classrooms." *Australian Journal of Teacher Education* 43 (2): 116–42.

Bryant, R. A., and P. Panasetis. 2001. "Panic Symptoms During Trauma and Acute Stress Disorder." *Behaviour Research and Therapy* 39 (8): 961–66.

Bryk, A., and B. Schneider. 2003. "Trust in Schools: A Core Resource for School Reform." *Educational Leadership* 60 (6): 40–45.

Bundick, M. J. et al. 2021. "The Contours of Purpose Beyond the Self in Midlife and Later Life." *Applied Developmental Science* 25 (1): 62–82.

Burić, I., A. Slišković, and I. Sorić. 2020. "Teachers' Emotions and Self-Efficacy: A Test of Reciprocal Relations." *Frontiers in Psychology* 11: 1650.

Cantor, P. et al. 2019. "Malleability, Plasticity, and Individuality: How Children Learn and Develop in Context." *Applied Developmental Science* 23 (4): 307–37.

Caprara, G. V. et al. 2000. "Prosocial Foundations of Children's Academic Achievement." *Psychological Science* 11 (4): 302–6.

Chadwick, E.D., P. E. Jose, and F. B. Bryant. 2020. "Styles of Everyday Savoring Differentially Predict Well-Being in Adolescents over One Month." *Journal of Happiness Studies* 22: 803–24.

Chan, D. W. 2010. "Gratitude, Gratitude Intervention and Subjective Well-Being Among Chinese School Teachers in Hong Kong." *Educational Psychology* 30 (2): 139–53.

Chen, S. K., and M. Mongrain. 2020. "Awe and the Interconnected Self." *The Journal of Positive Psychology.* https://doi.org/10.1080/17439760.2020.1818808.

Chen, S., and C. H. Jordan. 2020. "Incorporating Ethics into Brief Mindfulness Practice: Effects on Well-Being and Prosocial Behavior." *Mindfulness* 11: 18–29.

Chin, M. J., D. M. Quinn, T. K. Dhaliwal, and V. S. Lovison. 2020. "Bias in the Air: A Nationwide Exploration of Teachers' Implicit Racial Attitudes, Aggregate Bias, and Student Outcomes." *Educational Researcher* 49 (8): 566–78.

Chirico, A. et al. 2018. "Awe Enhances Creative Thinking: An Experimental Study." *Creativity Research Journal* 30 (2): 123–31.

Cipriano, C., and M. Brackett. 2020. "How to Support Teachers' Emotional Needs Right Now." *Greater Good.* https://greatergood.berkeley.edu/article/item/ how_to_support_teachers_emotional_needs_right_now.

Clancy, F. et al. 2020. "The Association Between Worry and Rumination with Sleep in Non-Clinical Populations." *Health Psychology Review* 14 (4): 427–48.

Clark, P., and E. Zygmunt. 2014. "A Close Encounter with Personal Bias: Pedagogical Implications for Teacher Education." *Journal of Negro Education* 8 (2): 147–61.

Collins, B. 2001. "The Companionship of a Poem." *The Chronicle of Higher Education* 23: B5.

Compas, B. E. et al. 2017. "Coping, Emotion Regulation, and Psychopathology in Childhood and Adolescence." *Psychological Bulletin* 143 (9): 939–91.

Condon, P., and D. DeSteno. 2011. "Compassion for One Reduces Punishment for Another." *Journal of Experimental Social Psychology* 47 (3): 698–701.

Condon, P. et al. 2013. "Meditation Increases Compassion Responses to Suffering." *Psychological Science* 24 (10): 2125–27.

Cooper, J. E. 2007. "Strengthening the Case for Community-Based Learning in Teacher Education." *Journal of Teacher Education* 58 (3): 245–55.

Corbett, C., J. Egan, and M. Pilch. 2019. "A Randomised Comparison of Two 'Stress Control' Programmes: Progressive Muscle Relaxation Versus Mindfulness Body Scan." *Mental Health & Prevention* 15: 200163.

Crain, T. L., K. A. Schonert-Reichl, and R. W. Roeser. 2017. "Cultivating Teacher Mindfulness: Effects of a Randomized Controlled Trial on Work, Home, and Sleep Outcomes." *Journal of Occupational Health Psychology* 22 (2): 138–52.

Crenshaw, K. 1989. "Demarginalizing the Intersection of Race and Sex: A Black Feminist Critique of Antidiscrimination Doctrine, Feminist Theory, and Antiracist Politics." *University of Chicago Legal Forum* 1989 (1): 8.

Crossan, M., D. Mazutis, and G. Seijts. 2013. "In Search of Virtue: The Role of Virtues, Values, and Character Strengths in Ethical Decision Making." *Journal of Business Ethics* 113: 567–81.

Crowder, R. et al. 2020. "Art as Meditation: A Mindful Inquiry into Educator Well-Being." *The Qualitative Report* 25 (3): 876–90.

Csaszar, I. E., J. R. Curry, and R. E. Lastrapes. 2018. "Effects of Loving Kindness Meditation on Student Teachers' Reported Levels of Stress and Empathy." *Teacher Education Quarterly* 45 (4): 93–116.

Csikszentmihalyi, M. 2014. *The Systems Model of Creativity: The Collected Works of Mihalyi Csikszentmihalyi.* New York: Springer.

Curry, O. S. et al. 2018. "Happy to Help? A Systematic Review and Meta-Analysis of the Effects of Performing Acts of Kindness on the Well-Being of the Actor." *Journal of Experimental Social Psychology* 76: 320–29.

Cutrona, C. E., and J. A. Suhr. 1992. "Controllability of Stressful Events and Satisfaction with Spouse Support Behaviors." *Communication Research* 19 (2): 154–74.

Dahl, D. J., C. D. Wilson-Mendenhall, and R. J. Davidson. 2020. "The Plasticity of Well-Being." *Proceedings of the National Academy of Sciences* 117 (51): 32197–206.

Daks, J. S., and R. D. Rogge. 2020. "Examining the Correlates of Psychological Flexibility in Romantic Relationship and Family Dynamics." *Journal of Contextual Behavioral Science* 18: 214–38.

Damon, W., J. Mennon, and K. Bronk. 2003. "The Development of Purpose During Adolescence." *Applied Developmental Science* 7 (3): 19–128.

Daoud, N., and S. A. Parsons. 2021. "Visioning and Hope: A Longitudinal Study of Two Teachers from Preservice to Inservice." *Peabody Journal of Education* 96 (4): 393–405.

Datu, J. A. D., and N. Park. 2019. "Perceived School Kindness and Academic Engagement: The Mediational Roles of Achievement Goal Orientations." *School Psychology International* 40 (5): 456–73.

David, S. 2016. *Emotional Agility: Get Unstuck, Embrace Change, and Thrive in Work and Life.* London: Penguin Life.

Deci, E. L., and R. M. Ryan. 2012. "Self-Determination Theory." In *Handbook of Theories of Social Psychology,* edited by P. A. M. Van Lange, A. W. Kruglanski, and E. T. Higgins. Los Angeles: Sage.

Denworth, L. 2020. *Friendship: The Evolution, Biology, and Extraordinary Power of Life's Fundamental Bond.* New York: W. W. Norton.

Dixson, D. D. et al. 2018. "The Magic of Hope: Hope Mediates the Relationship Between Socioeconomic Status and Academic Achievement." *The Journal of Educational Research* 111 (4): 507–15.

Donald, J. N. et al. 2019. "Does Your Mindfulness Benefit Others? A Systematic Review and Meta-Analysis of the Link Between Mindfulness and Prosocial Behaviour." *British Journal of Psychology* 110 (1): 101–25.

Donker, M. H. et al. 2020. "Teachers' Emotional Exhaustion: Associations with Their Typical Use of and Implicit Attitudes Toward Emotion Regulation Strategies." *Frontiers in Psychology* 11: 867.

Dorado, J., and V. Zakrzewski. 2013. "How to Help a Traumatized Child in the Classroom." *Greater Good.* https://greatergood.berkeley.edu/article/item/the_silent_epidemic_in_our_classrooms.

Dorado, J. et al. 2016. "Healthy Environments and Response to Trauma in Schools (HEARTS)." *School Mental Health* 8: 163–76.

Dunne, S., D. Sheffield, and J. Chilcot. 2018. "Brief Report: Self-Compassion, Physical Health, and the Mediating Role of Health-Promoting Behaviours." *Journal of Health Psychology* 23 (7): 993–99.

Dweck, C. 2014. "Teachers' Mindsets: 'Every Student Has Something to Teach Me': Feeling Overwhelmed? Where Did Your Natural Teaching Talent Go? Try Pairing a Growth Mindset with Reasonable Goals, Patience, and Reflection Instead. It's Time to Get Gritty and Be a Better Teacher." *Educational Horizons* 93 (2): 10–15.

Egan, K. 2014. "Wonder, Awe, and Teaching Techniques." In *Wonder-Full Education: The Centrality of Wonder in Teaching and Learning Across the Curriculum,* edited by K. Egan, A. Cant, and G. Judson. New York: Routledge.

Eggenberger, A. L. B. 2021. "Active Listening Skills as Predictors of Success in Community College Students." *Community College Journal of Research and Practice* 45 (5): 324–33.

Eldor, L., and A. Shoshani. 2016. "Caring Relationships in School Staff: Exploring the Link Between Compassion and Teacher Work Engagement." *Teaching and Teacher Education* 59: 126–36.

Emerson, L. M. et al. 2017. "Teaching Mindfulness to Teachers." *Mindfulness* 8: 1136–49.

Emmons, R. E. 2007. *Thanks! How Practicing Gratitude Can Make You Happier.* New York: Houghton Mifflin.

Eva, A., C. Bemis, M. Feris-Quist, and B. Hollands. 2014. "The Power of the Poetic Lens: Why Teachers Need to Read Poems Together." *JAEPL* 19: 62–73.

Eyal, T. et al. 2009. "When Values Matter: Expressing Values in Behavioral Intentions for the Near Vs. Distant Future." *Journal of Experimental Social Psychology* 45 (1): 35–43.

Eyal, T., M. Steffel, and N. Epley. 2018. "Perspective Mistaking: Accurately Understanding the Mind of Another Requires Getting Perspective, not Taking Perspective." *Journal of Personality and Social Psychology* 114 (4): 547–71.

Farb, N. et al. 2015. "Interoception, Contemplative Practice, and Health." *Frontiers in Psychology* 6: 763.

Farouk, S. 2010: "Primary School Teachers' Restricted and Elaborated Anger." *Cambridge Journal of Education* 40 (4): 353–68.

Feldman, D. B., M. Balaraman, and C. Anderson. 2018. "Hope and Meaning-In-Life: Points of Contact Between Hope Theory and Existentialism." In *The Oxford Handbook of Hope,* edited by M. W. Gallagher and S. J. Lopez. New York: Oxford University Press.

Feldman, D. B., and D. E. Dreher. 2012. "Can Hope Be Changed in 90 Minutes? Testing the Efficacy of a Single-Session Goal-Pursuit Intervention for College Students." *Journal of Happiness Studies* 13: 745–59.

Finnegan, K. S., and A. J. Daly. 2017. "The Trust Gap: Understanding the Effects of Leadership Churn in School Districts." *American Educator* 41 (2): 24–29.

Fiorilli, C. et al. 2019. "Teachers' Burnout: The Role of Trait Emotional Intelligence and Social Support." *Frontiers in Psychology* 10: 2743.

Fischer, D., M. Messner, and O. Pollatos. 2017. "Improvement of Interoceptive Processes After an Eight-Week Body Scan Intervention." *Frontiers in Human Neuroscience* 11: 452.

Fisher-Borne, M., J. M. Cain, and S. L. Martin. 2015. "From Mastery to Accountability: Cultural Humility as an Alternative to Cultural Competence." *Social Work Education* 34 (2): 165–81.

Flook, L., S. B. Goldberg, L. Pinger, and R. J. Davidson. 2015. "Promoting Prosocial Behavior and Self-Regulatory Skills in Preschool Children Through a Mindfulness-Based Kindness Curriculum." *Developmental Psychology* 51 (1): 44–51.

Fogelman, N., and T. Canli. 2015. "'Purpose in Life' as a Psychosocial Resource in Healthy Aging." *Nature Partner Journals: Aging and Mechanisms of Disease.* https://www.nature.com/articles/npjamd20156/fig_tab.

Ford, B. Q., and J. J. Gross. 2019. "Why Beliefs About Emotion Matter." *Current Directions in Psychological Science* 28 (1): 74–81.

Foronda, C., D. Baptiste, and M. M. Reinholdt. 2016. "Cultural Humility: A Concept Analysis." *Journal of Transcultural Nursing* 27 (3): 210–17.

Frank, J. L., D. Reibel et al. 2015. "The Effectiveness of Mindfulness-Based Stress Reduction on Educator Stress and Well-Being." *Mindfulness* 6: 208–16.

Fredrickson, B. L. 2001. "The Role of Positive Emotions in Positive Psychology." *American Psychologist* 56 (3): 218–26.

Fredrickson, B. L., and M. F. Losada. 2005. "Positive Affect and Complex Dynamics of Human Flourishing." *American Psychologist* 60 (7): 678–86.

Freeman, M. 2015. "Beholding and Being Beheld: Simone Weil, Iris Murdoch, and the Ethics of Attention." *The Humanistic Psychologist* 43 (2): 160–72.

Frenzel, A. C. et al. 2009. "Emotional Transmission in the Classroom." *Journal of Educational Psychology* 101 (3): 705–16.

Futterman Collier, A., and H. A. Wayment. 2021. "Enhancing and Explaining Art-Making for Mood-Repair." *Psychology of Aesthetics, Creativity, and the Arts* 15 (2): 363–75.

Galla, B. M., and A. L. Duckworth. 2015. "More than Resisting Temptation: Beneficial Habits Mediate the Relationship Between Self-Control and Positive Life Outcomes." *Journal of Personality and Social Psychology* 109 (3): 508–25.

Gard, T. et al. 2011. "Pain Attenuation Through Mindfulness Is Associated with Decreased Cognitive Control and Increased Sensory Processing in the Brain." *Cerebral Cortex* 22 (11): 2692–702.

Gerend, M., and J. Maner. 2011. "Fear, Anger, Fruits, and Veggies: Interactive Effects of Emotion and Message Framing on Health Behavior." *Health Psychology* 30: 420–23.

Ghobari Bonab, B. et al. 2020. "Effectiveness of Forgiveness Education with Adolescents in Reducing Anger and Ethnic Prejudice in Iran." *Journal of Educational Psychology.* https://doi.org/10.1037/edu0000622.

Gilbert, P. 2009. *The Compassionate Mind: A New Approach to Life's Challenges.* Oakland, CA: New Harbinger.

Ginwright, S. 2015. *Hope and Healing in Urban Education: How Teachers and Activists Are Reclaiming Matters of the Heart.* New York: Routledge.

Ginwright, S. 2018. "The Future of Healing: Shifting from Trauma-Informed Care to Healing-Centered Engagement." *Medium.* https://medium.com/@ginwright/the-future-of-healing-shifting-from-trauma -informed-care-to-healing-centered-engagement-634f557ce69c.

Goetz, J. L., D. Keltner, and E. Simon-Thomas. 2010. "Compassion: An Evolutionary Analysis and Empirical Review." *Psychological Bulletin* 136 (3): 351–74.

Goldin, P. R., and J. J. Gross. 2010. "Effects of Mindfulness-Based Stress Reduction (MBSR) on Emotion Regulation in Social Anxiety Disorder." *Emotion* 10 (1): 83–91.

Goleman, D. 2006. *Social Intelligence: The New Science of Human Relationships.* New York: Bantam.

Goodall, J., and C. Montgomery. 2014. "Parental Involvement to Parental Engagement: A Continuum." *Educational Review* 66 (4): 399–410.

Gorski, P. C. 2011. "Unlearning Deficit Ideology and the Scornful Gaze: Thoughts on Authenticating the Class Discourse in Education." *Counterpoints* 402: 152–73.

Goyer, J. P. et al. 2019. "Targeted Identity-Safety Interventions Cause Lasting Reductions in Discipline Citations Among Negatively Stereotyped Boys." *Journal of Personality and Social Psychology* 117: 1–31.

Green, T. L. 2017. "Community-Based Equity Audits: A Practical Approach for Educational Leaders to Support Equitable Community-School Improvements." *Educational Administration Quarterly* 53 (1): 3–39.

Gross, J. J. 1998. "The Emerging Field of Emotion Regulation: An Integrative Review." *Review of General Psychology* 2 (3): 271–99.

Gruber, M. J., B. D. Gelman, and C. Ranganath. 2014. "States of Curiosity Modulate Hippocampus-Dependent Learning via the Dopaminergic Circuit." *Neuron* 84 (2): 486–96.

Han, J., and H. Yin. 2016. "Teacher Motivation: Definition, Research Development, and Implications for Teachers." *Cogent Education* 3 (1): 1217819.

Hanson, R., and R. Mendius. 2009. *Buddha's Brain: The Practical Neuroscience of Happiness, Love, and Wisdom.* Oakland, CA: New Harbinger.

Harbaugh, W. T., U. Mayr, and D. R. Burghart. 2007. "Neural Responses to Taxation and Voluntary Giving Reveal Motives for Charitable Donations." *Science* 316 (5831): 1622–25.

Harzer, C., and W. Ruch. 2012. "When the Job Is a Calling: The Role of Applying One's Signature Strengths at Work." *Journal of Positive Psychology* 7: 362–71.

Haydon, T. et al. 2019. "'Check Yourself': Mindfulness-Based Stress Reduction for Teachers of Students with Challenging Behaviors." *Beyond Behavior* 28 (1): 55–60.

He, Y. 2009. "Strength-Based Mentoring in Pre-Service Teacher Education." *Mentoring & Tutoring: Partnership in Learning* 17 (3): 263–75.

Heeren, A., and P. Philippot. 2011. "Changes in Ruminative Thinking Mediate the Clinical Benefits of Mindfulness." *Mindfulness* 2 (1): 8–13.

Herman, J. 2015. *Trauma and Recovery: The Aftermath of Violence—from Domestic Abuse to Political Terror.* New York: Basic Books.

Hill, P. L., and N. A. Turiano. 2014. "Purpose in Life as a Predictor of Mortality Across Adulthood." *Psychological Science* 25 (7): 1482–86.

Hirshberg, M. J. et al. 2020. "Integrating Mindfulness and Connection Practices into Preservice Teacher Education Improves Classroom Practices." *Learning and Instruction* 66: 101298.

Hochschild, A. R. 1983. *The Managed Heart: Commercialization of Human Feeling.* Berkeley: University of California Press.

Hofmann, S. G. et al. 2012. "The Efficacy of Cognitive Behavioral Therapy." *Cognitive Therapy and Research* 36 (5): 427–40.

Hölzel, B. K. et al. 2011. "Mindfulness Practice Leads to Increases in Regional Brain Gray Matter Density." *Psychiatry Research: Neuroimaging* 191 (1): 36–43.

Hook, J. N., and D. E. Davis. 2019. "Cultural Humility: Introduction to the Special Issue." *Journal of Psychology and Theology* 47 (2): 71–75.

Hopper, E. 2016. "Spending Money on Others Can Lower Your Blood Pressure." *Greater Good.* https://greatergood.berkeley.edu/article/item/spending_money_on_others_can_lower_your_blood_pressure.

Howells, K., and J. Cumming. 2012. "Exploring the Role of Gratitude in the Professional Experience of Pre-Service Teachers." *Teaching Education* 23 (1): 71–88.

Iancu, A. et al. 2018. "The Effectiveness of Interventions Aimed at Reducing Teacher Burnout." *Educational Psychology Review* 30: 373–96.

Ingram, M. A. 2003. "When I Dream of Paris: How Sociocultural Poetry Can Assist Psychotherapy Practitioners to Understand and Affirm the Lived Experiences of Members of Oppressed Groups." *Journal of Poetry Therapy* 16 (4): 221–27.

Izard, C. E. 2011. "Forms and Functions of Emotions: Matters of Emotion-Cognition Interactions." *Emotion Review* 3 (4): 371–78.

Janik, M., and S. Rothmann. 2015. "Meaningful Work and Secondary School Teachers' Intention to Leave." *South African Journal of Education* 35 (2): 1008.

Jacques, C., and A. Villegas. 2018. *Strategies for Equitable Family Engagement.* Washington, DC: State Support Network.

Jazaieri, H. et al. 2014. "A Randomized Controlled Trial of Compassion Cultivation Training: Effects on Mindfulness, Affect, and Emotion Regulation." *Motivation and Emotion* 38 (1): 23–35.

Jennings, P. A. 2008. "Contemplative Education and Youth Development." *New Directions for Youth Development* 118: 101–5.

———. 2015. "Early Childhood Teachers' Well-Being, Mindfulness, and Self-Compassion in Relation to Classroom Quality and Attitudes Towards Challenging Students." *Mindfulness* 6 (4): 732–43.

Jennings, P. A., and M. T. Greenberg. 2009. "The Prosocial Classroom: Teacher Social and Emotional Competence in Relation to Student and Classroom Outcomes." *Review of Educational Research* 79 (1): 491–525.

Jennings, P. A. et al. 2013. "Improving Classroom Learning Environments by Cultivating Awareness and Resilience in Education (CARE)." *School Psychology Quarterly* 28 (4): 374–90.

Jennings, P. A. et al. 2017. "Impacts of the CARE for Teachers Program on Teachers' Social and Emotional Competence and Classroom Interactions." *Journal of Educational Psychology* 109 (7): 1010–28.

Jin, G. C., and Y. Z. Wang. 2019. "The Influence of Gratitude on Learning Engagement Among Adolescents." *Journal of Adolescence* 77: 21–31.

Johnson J. et al. 2017. "Resilience to Emotional Distress in Response to Failure, Error or Mistakes." *Clinical Psychology Review* 52: 19–42.

Jones, S. M., G. D. Bodie, and S. D. Hughes. 2019. "The Impact of Mindfulness on Empathy, Active Listening, and Perceived Provisions of Emotional Support." *Communication Research* 46 (6): 838–65.

Jung, H. et al. 2020. "Prosocial Modeling: A Meta-Analytic Review and Synthesis." *Psychological Bulletin* 146 (8): 635–63.

Juvonen, J., K. Kogachi, and S. Graham. 2018. "When and How Do Students Benefit from Ethnic Diversity in Middle School?" *Child Development* 89 (4): 1268–82.

Kang, Y., J. R. Gray, and J. F. Dovidio. 2014. "The Nondiscriminating Heart: Lovingkindness Meditation Training Decreases Implicit Intergroup Bias." *Journal of Experimental Psychology: General* 143 (3): 1306–13.

Kashdan, T. B., L. F. Barrett, and P. E. McNight. 2015. "Unpacking Emotion Differentiation: Transforming Unpleasant Experience by Perceiving Distinctions in Negativity." *Current Directions in Psychological Science* 24 (1): 10–16.

Kashdan, T., and R. Biwas-Diener. 2014. *The Upside of Your Dark Side: Why Being Your Whole Self—Not Just Your "Good" Self—Drives Success and Fulfillment.* New York: Penguin.

Kashdan. T. et al. 2013. "How Are Curious People Viewed and How Do They Behave in Social Situations?" *Journal of Personality* 81 (2): 142–54.

Kashdan, T. et al. 2018. "The Five-Dimensional Curiosity Scale: Capturing the Bandwidth of Curiosity and Identifying Four Unique Subgroups of Curious People." *Journal of Research in Personality* 73: 130–49.

Katz, D. A. et al. 2018. "Educators' Emotion Regulation Strategies and Their Physiological Indicators of Chronic Stress Over One Year." *Stress and Health* 34: 278–85.

Keeley, J., D. Smith, and W. Buskist. 2006. "The Teacher Behaviors Checklist: Factor Analysis of Its Utility for Evaluating Teaching." *Teaching of Psychology* 33: 84–91.

Keels, M., M. Durkee, and E. Hope. 2017. "The Psychological and Academic Costs of School-Based Racial and Ethnic Microaggressions." *American Educational Research Journal* 54 (6): 1316–44.

Keltner, D. 2016a. *The Power Paradox: How We Gain and Lose Influence.* New York: Penguin.

———. 2016b. "Why Do We Feel Awe?" *Greater Good.* https://greatergood.berkeley.edu/article/item/why_do_we_feel_awe.

Keltner, D., and J. Haidt. 2001. "Social Functions of Emotions." In *Emotions: Current Issues and Future Directions,* edited by T. J. Mayne and G. A Bonanno. New York: Guilford Press.

Kettler, T., K. N. Lamb, A. Willerson, and D. R. Mullet. 2018. "Teachers' Perceptions of Creativity in the Classroom." *Creativity Research Journal* 30 (2): 164–71.

Kidd, D. C., and E. Castana. 2013. "Reading Fiction Improves Theory of Mind." *Science* 342 (6156): 377–80.

Killingsworth, M. A., and D. T. Gilbert. 2010. "A Wandering Mind Is an Unhappy Mind." *Science* 330 (6006): 932.

Kimhi, Y., and L. Geronik. 2020. "Creativity Promotion in an Excellence Program for Preservice Teacher Candidates." *Journal of Teacher Education* 71 (5): 505–17.

Kinman, G., S. Wray, and C. Strange. 2011. "Emotional Labour, Burnout, and Job Satisfaction in UK Teachers." *Educational Psychology* 31 (7): 843–56.

Kirby, J. N., C. L. Tellegen, and S. R. Steindl. 2017. "A Meta-Analysis of Compassion-Based Interventions." *Behavior Therapy* 48 (6): 778–92.

Klassen, R. M., and M. M. Chiu. 2010. "Effects on Teachers' Self-Efficacy and Job Satisfaction: Teacher Gender, Years of Experience, and Job Stress." *Journal of Educational Psychology* 102 (3): 741–56.

Klassen, R., and T. Durksen. 2014. "Weekly Self-Efficacy and Work Stress of Pre-Service Teachers During the Final Teaching Practicum." *Learning and Instruction* 33: 158–69.

Klimecki, O. 2019. "The Role of Empathy and Compassion in Conflict Resolution." *Emotion Review* 11 (4): 310–25.

Klimecki, O. et al. 2013. "Functional Neural Plasticity and Associated Changes in Positive Affect After Compassion Training." *Cerebral Cortex* 23 (7): 1552–61.

Klimecki, O., and T. Singer. 2011. "Empathic Distress Fatigue Rather than Compassion Fatigue? Integrating Findings from Empathy Research in Psychology and Social Neuroscience." In *Pathological Altruism,* edited by B. Oakley, A. Knafo, G. Madhavan, and D. S. Wilson. Oxford: Oxford University Press.

Klingbeil, D. A., and T. L. Renshaw. 2018. "Mindfulness-Based Interventions for Teachers." *School Psychology Quarterly* 3 (4): 501–11.

Koutouzis, M., and K. Spyriadou. 2017. "The Interaction Between Professional and Social Identity in Greek Primary School Teachers." *International Journal of Education* 9 (4): 190–209.

Kramer, A. D., J. E. Guillory, and J. T. Hancock. 2014. "Experimental Evidence of Massive-Scale Emotional Contagion Through Social Networks." *PNAS* 111 (24): 8788–90.

Kross, E. et al. 2014. "Self-Talk as a Regulatory Mechanism: How You Do It Matters." *Journal of Personality and Social Psychology* 106 (2): 304–24.

Kuo, M., M. Barnes, and C. Jordan. 2019. "Do Experiences with Nature Promote Learning?" *Frontiers in Psychology* 10: 305.

Kuo, M., M. Browning, and M. L. Penner. 2018. "Do Lessons in Nature Boost Subsequent Classroom Engagement? Refueling Students in Flight." *Frontiers in Psychology* 8: 2253.

Lambert, S. F. et al. 2009. "Perceptions of Racism and Depressive Symptoms in African American Adolescents." *Journal of Youth and Adolescence* 38 (4): 519–31.

Lamm, C., J. Decety, and T. Singer. 2011. "Meta-Analytic Evidence for Common and Distinct Neural Networks Associated with Directly Experienced Pain and Empathy for Pain." *Neuroimage* 54 (3), 2492–502.

Lasater, K., T. C. Crowe, and J. Pijanowski. 2021. "Developing Family-School Partnerships in the Midst of Demographic Change: An Examination of Educators' Attitudes, Values, and Beliefs and the Discourses They Shape." *Leadership and Policy in Schools.* https://doi.org/10.1080/15700763.2021.1958869.

Lavelle Heineberg, B. D. 2016. "Promoting Caring: Mindfulness- and Compassion-Based Contemplative Training for Educators and Students." In *Handbook of Mindfulness in Education: Integrating Theory and Research into Practice,* edited by K. A. Schonert-Reichl and R. W. Roeser. New York: Springer.

Lavelock, C. R. et al. 2014. "The Quiet Virtue Speaks: An Intervention to Promote Humility." *Journal of Psychology and Theology* 42 (1): 99–110.

Lavy, S., and A. Berkovich-Ohana. 2020. "From Teachers' Mindfulness to Students' Thriving: The Mindful Self in School Relationships (MSSR) Model." *Mindfulness* 11: 2258–73.

Lavy, S., and E. Naama-Ghanayim. 2020. "Why Care About Caring? Linking Teachers' Caring and Sense of Meaning at Work with Students' Self-Esteem, Well-Being, and School Engagement." *Teaching and Teacher Education* 91: 103046.

Layous, K. et al. 2012. "Kindness Counts: Prompting Prosocial Behavior in Preadolescents Boosts Peer Acceptance and Well-Being." *PLoS ONE* 7 (12): e51380.

Lazarus, R. S., and S. Folkman. 1984. *Stress, Appraisal, and Coping.* New York: Springer.

Lee, A. H., and R. DiGiuseppe. 2017. "Anger and Aggression Treatments." *Current Opinion in Psychology* 19: 65–74.

Lee, J. et al. 2014. "Influence of Forest Therapy on Cardiovascular Relaxation in Young Adults." *Evidence-Based Complementary and Alternative Medicine* 2014: 834360.

Lee, M. et al. 2016. "Teachers' Emotions and Emotion Management: Integrating Emotion Regulation Theory with Emotional Labor Research." *Social Psychology of Education* 19: 843–63.

Leiberg, S., O. Klimecki, and T. Singer. 2011. "Short-Term Compassion Training Increases Prosocial Behavior in a Newly Developed Prosocial Game." *PLoS ONE* 6 (3): e17798.

Leis, M. et al. 2017. "Leading Together: Strengthening Relational Trust in the Adult School Community." *Journal of School Leadership* 27 (6): 831–59.

Leonard J. A., Y. Lee, and L. E. Schulz. 2017. "Infants Make More Attempts to Achieve a Goal When They See Adults Persist." *Science* 357 (6357): 1290–94.

Levine, M., A. Prosser, D. Evans, and S. Reicher. 2005. "Identity and Emergency Intervention: How Social Group Membership and Inclusiveness of Group Boundaries Shape Helping Behavior." *Personality and Social Psychology Bulletin* 31 (4): 443–53.

Lewis, N. A., N. A. Turiano, B. R. Payne, and P. L. Hill. 2017. "Purpose in Life and Cognitive Functioning in Adulthood." *Aging, Neuropsychology, and Cognition* 24 (6): 662–71.

Liauw, I. et al. 2018. "Gratitude for Teachers as a Psychological Resource for Early Adolescents." *Journal of Moral Education* 47 (4): 397–414.

Lieberman, M. D. et al. 2007. "Putting Feelings into Words: Affective Labeling Disrupts Amygdala Activity in Response to Affective Stimuli." *Psychological Science* 18 (5): 421–28.

Linden, D. L. 2015. *Touch: The Science of the Hand, Heart, and Mind.* New York: Penguin.

Littman-Ovadia, H., and D. Nir. 2014. "Looking Forward to Tomorrow: The Buffering Effect of a Daily Optimism Intervention." *The Journal of Positive Psychology* 9 (2): 122–36.

Llewellyn, N. et al. 2013. "Reappraisal and Suppression Mediate the Contribution of Regulatory Focus to Anxiety in Healthy Adults." *Emotion* 13 (4): 610–15.

Lomas, T. et al. 2017. "The Impact of Mindfulness on Well-Being and Performance in the Workplace." *European Journal of Work and Organizational Psychology* 26 (4): 492–513.

Luberto, C. M. et al. 2018. "A Systematic Review and Meta-Analysis of the Effects of Meditation on Empathy, Compassion, and Prosocial Behaviors." *Mindfulness* 9: 708–24.

Lueke, A., and B. Gibson. 2014. "Mindfulness Meditation Reduces Implicit Age and Race Bias: The Role of Reduced Automaticity of Responding." *Social Psychological and Personality Science* 6 (3): 1–8.

Lund, D. E., and L. Lee. 2015. "Fostering Cultural Humility Among Pre-Service Teachers: Connecting with Children and Youth of Immigrant Families Through Service-Learning." *Canadian Journal of Education* 38 (2): 1–30.

Luthar, S. S., and S. H. Mendes. 2020. "Trauma-Informed Schools: Supporting Educators as They Support the Children." *International Journal of School and Educational Psychology* 8 (2): 147–57.

Lutz, A., J. Brefczynski-Lewis, T. Johnstone, and R. J. Davidson. 2008. "Regulation of the Neural Circuitry of Emotion by Compassion Meditation: Effects of Meditative Expertise." *PLoS ONE* 3 (3): e1897.

Mackenzie, E. R. et al. 2020. "Present-Moment Awareness and the Prosocial Classroom: Educators' Lived Experience of Mindfulness." *Mindfulness* 11: 2755–64.

Magee, R. 2019. *The Inner Work of Racial Justice.* New York: TarcherPerigree.

Mahler, D., J. Großschedl, and U. Harms. 2018. "Does Motivation Matter? The Relationship Between Teachers' Self-Efficacy and Enthusiasm and Students' Performance." *PloS One* 13 (11): e0207252.

Majer, M. et al. 2010. "Association of Childhood Trauma with Cognitive Function in Healthy Adults." *BMC Neurology* 10: 61.

Majid, R. 2014. "Teacher Character Strengths and Talent Development." *International Education Studies* 7 (13): 175–83.

Malin, H. 2018. *Teaching with Purpose: Preparing Students for Lives of Meaning.* Cambridge, MA: Harvard University Press.

Mapp, K., and P. Kuttner. 2013. *Partners in Education: A Dual Capacity-Building Framework for Family-School Partnerships.* Austin, TX: Southwest Educational Development Laboratory in Association with the US Department of Education. https://www2.ed.gov/documents/family-community/partners-education.pdf.

Mar, R. A., K. Oatley, and J. B. Peterson. 2009. "Exploring the Link Between Reading Fiction and Empathy: Ruling Out Individual Differences and Examining Outcomes." *Communications* 34: 407–28.

Maslach, C., and M. P. Leiter. 2016. "Understanding the Burnout Experience: Recent Research and Its Implications for Psychiatry." *World Psychiatry* 15 (2): 103–11.

Mazzucchelli, T. G., R. T. Kane, and C. S. Rees. 2010. "Behavioral Activation Interventions for Well-Being." *The Journal of Positive Psychology* 5 (2): 105–21.

McCullough, M. E. et al. 2007. "Rumination, Fear, and Cortisol: An In Vivo Study of Interpersonal Transgressions." *Health Psychology* 26 (1): 126–32.

McGovern, T. V., and S. L. Miller. 2008. "Integrating Teacher Behaviors with Character Strengths and Virtues for Faculty Development." *Teaching of Psychology* 35 (4): 278–85.

McKay, L., and G. Barton. 2018. "Exploring How Arts-Based Reflection Can Support Teachers' Resilience and Well-Being." *Teaching and Teacher Education* 75: 356–65.

McLennan, B., P. McIlveen, and H. N. Perera. 2017. "Pre-Service Teachers' Self-Efficacy Mediates the Relationship Between Career Adaptability and Career Optimism." *Teaching and Teacher Education* 63: 176–85.

McPhetres, J. 2019. "Oh, the Things You Don't Know: Awe Promotes Awareness of Knowledge Gaps and Science Interest." *Cognition and Emotion* 33 (8): 1599–615.

Medvedev, O. N., S. D. Pratscher, and A. Bettencourt. 2020. "Psychometric Evaluation of the Interpersonal Mindfulness Scale Using Rasch Analysis." *Mindfulness* 11: 2007–15.

Meloy-Miller, K. C. 2018. "Anger Can Help: Clinical Representation of Three Pathways of Anger." *The American Journal of Family Therapy* 46 (1): 44–66.

Memarian, N. et al. 2017. "Neural Activity During Affect Labeling Predicts Expressive Writing Effects on Well-Being: GLM and SVM Approaches." *Social Cognitive and Affective Neuroscience* 12 (9): 1437–47.

Mesler, R. M., C. M. Corbin, and B. H. Martin. 2021. "Teacher Mindset Is Associated with Development of Students' Growth Mindset." *Journal of Applied Developmental Psychology* 76: 101299.

Minkkinen, J., E. Auvinen, and S. Mauno. 2020. "Meaningful Work Protects Teachers' Self-Rated Health Under Stressors." *Journal of Positive School Psychology* 4 (2): 140–52.

Morelli, S. A., M. D. Lieberman, and J. Zaki. 2015. "The Emerging Study of Positive Empathy." *Social and Personality Psychology Compass* 9 (2): 57–68.

Morgan, J., and L. Atkin. 2016. "Expelling Stress for Primary School Teachers: Self-Affirmation Increases Positive Emotions in Teaching and Emotion Reappraisal." *International Journal of Environmental Research and Public Health* 13 (5): 500.

Mullen, B., M. M. Migdal, and D. Rozell. 2003. "Self-Awareness, Deindividuation, and Social Identity: Unraveling Theoretical Paradoxes by Filling Empirical Lacunae." *Personality and Social Psychology Bulletin* 29 (9): 1071–81.

Musick, M. A., and J. Wilson. 2003. "Volunteering and Depression." *Social Science and Medicine* 56 (2): 259–69.

Nasser, I. and M. Abu-Nimer. 2012. "Perceptions of Forgiveness Among Palestinian Teachers in Israel." *Journal of Peace Education* 9 (1): 1–15.

National Child Traumatic Stress Network. 2011. *Secondary Traumatic Stress: A Fact Sheet for Child-Serving Professionals.* Los Angeles: National Center for Child Traumatic Stress.

National Scientific Council on the Developing Child. 2015. *Supportive Relationships and Active Skill-Building Strengthen the Foundations of Resilience: Working Paper No. 13.* https://developingchild.harvard.edu/resources/supportive-relationships-and-active-skill-building-strengthen-the-foundations-of-resilience.

Neff, K. 2011. *Self-Compassion: The Proven Power of Being Kind to Yourself.* New York: HarperCollins.

Neff, K., and C. K. Germer. 2013. "A Pilot Study and Randomized Controlled Trial of the Mindful Self-Compassion Program." *Journal of Clinical Psychology* 69 (1): 28–44.

Neff, K., and E. Pommier. 2013. "The Relationship Between Self-Compassion and Other-Focused Concern Among College Undergraduates, Community Adults, and Practicing Meditators." *Self and Identity* 12 (2): 160–76.

Neuenschwander, R., A. Friedman-Krauss, C. Raver, and C. Blair. 2017. "Teacher Stress Predicts Child Executive Function: Moderation by School Poverty." *Early Education and Development* 28 (7): 880–900.

Niemiec, R. M. 2013. "VIA Character Strengths." In *Cross-Cultural Advancements in Positive Psychology,* vol. 3, *Well-Being and Cultures,* edited by H. Knoop and F. A. Delle. Dordrecht, Netherlands: Springer.

Nook, E. C., D. C. Ong, S. A. Morelli, J. P. Mitchell, and J. Zaki. 2016. "Prosocial Conformity: Prosocial Norms Generalize Across Behavior and Empathy." *Personality and Social Psychology Bulletin* 42 (8): 1045–62.

Norcross, J. C., M. S. Mrykalo, and M. D. Blagys. 2002. "Auld Lang Syne: Success Predictors, Change Processes, and Self-Reported Outcomes of New Year's Resolvers and Nonresolvers." *Journal of Clinical Psychology* 58 (4): 397–405.

Norcross, J. C., and J. D. Guy. 2007. *Leaving It at the Office: A Guide to Psychotherapist Self-Care.* New York: Guilford Press.

Oberle, E., and K. A. Schonert-Reichl. 2016. "Stress Contagion in the Classroom? The Link Between Classroom Teacher Burnout and Morning Cortisol in Elementary School Students." *Social Science & Medicine* 159: 30–37.

Okonofua, J., and J. L. Eberhardt. 2015. "Two Strikes: Race and the Disciplining of Young Students." *Psychological Science* 26: 617–24.

Orbell, S., and P. Sheeran. 2000. "Motivational and Volitional Processes in Action Initiation." *Journal of Applied Social Psychology* 30 (4): 780–97.

Orkibi, H. et al. 2018. "Pathways to Adolescents' Flourishing: Linking Self-Control Skills and Positivity Ratio Through Social Support." *Youth & Society* 50 (1): 3–25.

Osher, D. et al. 2020. "Drivers of Human Development: How Relationships and Context Shape Learning and Development." *Applied Developmental Science* 24 (1): 6–36.

Otake, K. et al. 2006. "Happy People Become Happier Through Kindness." *Journal of Happiness Studies* 7: 361–75.

Oyler, D. L. et al. 2021. "Mindfulness and Intergroup Bias." *Group Processes & Intergroup Relations*. https://doi.org/10.1177/1368430220978694.

Ozbay, F. et al. 2007. "Social Support and Resilience to Stress: From Neurobiology to Clinical Practice." *Psychiatry (Edgmont)* 4 (5): 35–40.

Pace, T. W. W. et al. 2009. "Effect of Compassion Meditation on Neuroendocrine, Innate, Immune, and Behavioral Responses to Psychosocial Stress." *Psychoneuroendocrinology* 34 (1): 87–98.

Paek, S. H., and S. E. Sumners. 2019. "The Indirect Effect of Teachers' Creative Mindsets on Teaching Creativity." *Journal of Creative Behavior* 53: 298–311.

Palmer, P. J. 2003. "Teaching with Heart and Soul: Reflections on Spirituality in Teacher Education." *Journal of Teacher Education* 54(5): 376–85.

Pang, V. O., and C. D. Park. 2003. "Examination of the Self-Regulation Mechanism: Prejudice Reduction in Pre-Service Teachers." *Action in Teacher Education* 25 (3): 1–12.

Park, B., E. Blevins, B. Knutson, and J. L. Tsai. 2017. "Neurocultural Evidence that Ideal Affect Promotes Giving." *Social Cognitive and Affective Neuroscience* 12: 1083–96.

Park, J., O. Ayduk, and E. Kross. 2016. "Stepping Back to Move Forward: Expressive Writing Promotes Self-Distancing." *Emotion* 16 (3): 349–64.

Parks, S., M. D. Birtel, and R. J. Crisp. 2017. "Evidence that a Brief Meditation Exercise Can Reduce Prejudice Towards Homeless People." *Social Psychology* 45: 458–65.

Parmentier, F. B. R. et al. 2019. "Mindfulness and Symptoms of Depression and Anxiety in the General Population." *Frontiers in Psychology* 10 (506): 1–10.

Pavey, L., T. Greitemeyer, and P. Sparks. 2011. "Highlighting Relatedness Promotes Prosocial Motives and Behavior." *Personality and Social Psychology Bulletin* 37 (7): 905–17.

Pelech, S., and D. Kelly. 2017. "'Surrendering to Curiosity': Impacts of Contemplation for Resisting Rationalized Experience in Teacher Education." *European Journal of Curriculum Studies* 4 (1): 570–83.

Penedo, F. J., and J. R. Dahn. 2005. "Exercise and Well-Being." *Current Opinions in Psychiatry* 18 (2): 189–93.

Pennebaker, J. W. 2018. "Expressive Writing in Psychological Science." *Perspectives on Psychological Science* 13 (2): 226–29.

Peterson, C., and M. Seligman. 2004. *Character Strengths and Virtues: A Handbook and Classification.* Washington, DC: American Psychological Association.

Phelps, P. H. 2000. "Mistakes as Vehicles for Educating Teachers." *Action in Teacher Education* 21 (4): 41–49.

Piff, P. K. et al. 2015. "Awe, the Small Self, and Prosocial Behavior." *Journal of Personality and Social Psychology* 108 (6): 883–99.

Pittinsky, T. L. 2016. "Why Overlook Microaffirmations?" *Phi Delta Kappan* 98 (2): 80–83.

Pittinsky, T. L., and R. M. Montoya. 2016. "Empathic Joy in Positive Intergroup Relations." *Journal of Social Issues* 72 (3): 511–23.

Porges, S. W. 2011. *The Polyvagal Theory: Neurophysiological Foundations of Emotions, Attachment, Communication, and Self-Regulation.* New York: W. W. Norton.

Powers, B., and P. B. Duffy. 2016. "Making Invisible Intersectionality Visible Through Theater of the Oppressed in Teacher Education." *Journal of Teacher Education* 67 (1): 61–73.

Pratscher, S. D., A. J. Rose, L. Markovitz, and A. Bettencourt. 2018. "Interpersonal Mindfulness: Investigating Mindfulness in Interpersonal Interactions, Co-Rumination, and Friendship Quality." *Mindfulness* 9 (4): 1206–15.

Pugach, M. C., J. Gomez-Najarro, and A. M. Matewos. 2019. "A Review of Identity in Research on Social Justice in Teacher Education: What Role for Intersectionality?" *Journal of Teacher Education* 70 (3): 206–18.

Quinn, B. P. 2016. "Learning from the Wisdom of Practice: Teachers' Educational Purposes as Pathways to Supporting Adolescent Purpose in Secondary Classrooms." *Journal of Education for Teaching* 42 (5): 602–23.

Quinn, D. M. 2017. "Racial Attitudes of PreK–12 and Postsecondary Educators." *Educational Researcher* 46 (7): 397–411.

Richardson, M., A. Cormack, L. McRobert, and R. Underhill. 2016. "Thirty Days Wild: Development and Evaluation of a Large-Scale Nature Engagement Campaign to Improve Well-Being." *PLoS ONE* 11 (2): e0149777.

Roemer, L., S. K. Williston, and L. G. Rollins. 2015. "Mindfulness and Emotional Regulation." *Current Opinion in Psychology* 3: 52–57.

Roeser, R. W. et al. 2013. "Mindfulness Training and Reductions in Teacher Stress and Burnout." *Journal of Educational Psychology* 105 (3): 787–804.

Roeser, R. W., and P. D. Zelazo. 2012. "Contemplative Science, Education, and Child Development." *Child Development Perspectives* 6: 143–45.

Rolstad, K., K. S. Mahoney, and G. V. Glass. 2005. "Weighing the Evidence: A Meta-Analysis of Bilingual Education in Arizona." *Bilingual Research Journal* 29 (1): 43–67.

Root, M. P. P. 1992. "Reconstructing the Impact of Trauma on Personality." In *Personality and Psychopathology: Feminist Reappraisals,* edited by L. S. Brown and M. Ballou. New York: Guilford Press.

Rosso, B. D., K. Dekas, and A. Wrzesniewski. 2010. "On the Meaning of Work: A Theoretical Integration and Review." *Research in Organizational Behavior* 30: 91–127.

Runco, M. A. 1991. *Divergent Thinking.* Norwood, NJ: Ablex.

Rusu, P. P., and A. A. Colomeischi. 2020. "Positivity Ratio and Well-Being Among Teachers. The Mediating Role of Work Engagement." *Frontiers in Psychology* 11: 1608.

Saleeby, D. 2008. "The Strengths Perspective: Putting Possibility and Hope to Work in Our Practice." In *The Profession of Social Work,* vol. 1, edited by B. W. White. Hoboken, NJ: John Wiley & Sons.

Salsman, J. M. 2019. "Effects of Psychosocial Interventions on Meaning and Purpose in Adults with Cancer: A Systematic Review and Meta-Analysis." *Cancer* 125 (14): 2383–93.

Santoro, D. 2018. *Demoralized: Why Teachers Leave the Profession They Love and How They Can Stay.* Cambridge, MA: Harvard Education Press.

Santos, R. G. et al. 2011. "Effectiveness of School-Based Violence Prevention for Children and Youth." *Healthcare Quarterly* 14 (2): 80–91.

Schreier, H. M. C., K. A. Schonert-Reichl, and E. Chen. 2013. "Effect of Volunteering on Risk Factors for Cardiovascular Disease in Adolescents." *JAMA Pediatrics* 167 (4): 327–32.

Schussler, D. L., P. A. Jennings, J. E. Sharp, and J. L. Frank. 2016. "Improving Teacher Awareness and Well-Being Through CARE." *Mindfulness* 7 (1): 130–42.

Schutte, N. S., and J. M. Malouff. 2019. "Increasing Curiosity Through Autonomy of Choice." *Motivation and Emotion* 43: 563–70.

———. 2020. "Connections Between Curiosity, Flow, and Creativity." *Personality and Individual Differences* 152: 10955.

Scida, E. E., and J. N. Jones. 2017. "Navigating Stress: Graduate Student Experiences with Contemplative Practices in a Foreign Language Teacher Education Course." *The Journal of Contemplative Inquiry* 4 (1): 207–28.

Seligman, M. E., T. A. Steen, N. Park, and C. Peterson. 2005. "Positive Psychology Progress: Empirical Validation of Interventions." *American Psychologist* 60 (5): 410.

Seligman, M., and M. Csikszentmihalyi. 2000. "Positive Psychology." *The American Psychologist* 55 (1): 5–14.

Sezgin, F., and O. Erdogan. 2015. "Academic Optimism, Hope, and Zest for Work as Predictors of Teacher Self-Efficacy and Perceived Success." *Educational Sciences: Theory and Practice* 15 (1): 7–19.

Shapiro, A. 2020. "'Interrupt the Systems': Robin DiAngelo on White Fragility and Anti-Racism." NPR. https://www.npr.org/2020/06/17/879136931/interrupt-the-systems-robin-diangelo-on-white-fragility-and-anti-racism.

Shapiro, S. L. et al. 2015. "Contemplation in the Classroom: A New Direction for Improving Childhood Education." *Educational Psychology Review* 27: 1–30.

Sheldon, K., P. Jose, T. Kashdan, and J. Aaron. 2015. "Personality, Effective Goal-Striving, and Enhanced Well-Being." *Personality & Social Psychology Bulletin* 41 (4): 575–85.

Shelton, S. A., and M. E. Barnes. 2016. "'Racism Just Isn't an Issue Anymore': Preservice Teachers' Resistances to the Intersections of Sexuality and Race." *Teaching and Teacher Education* 55: 165–74.

Sheridan, S. M. et al. 2019. "A Meta-Analysis of Family-School Interventions and Children's Social-Emotional Functioning." *Review of Educational Research* 89 (2): 296–332.

Shiota, M. N., D. Keltner, and A. Mossman. 2007. "The Nature of Awe: Elicitors, Appraisals, and Effects on Self-Concept." *Cognition and Emotion* 21 (5): 944–63.

Shonin, E. et al. 2015. "Buddhist-Derived Loving-Kindness and Compassion Meditation for the Treatment of Psychopathology." *Mindfulness* 6: 1161–80.

Siegel-Hawley, G. 2012. *How Non-Minority Students Also Benefit from Racially Diverse Schools. Research Brief #8.* Washington, DC: National Coalition on School Diversity.

Simmons, D., M. Brackett, and N. Adler. 2018. *Applying an Equity Lens to Social, Emotional, and Academic Development.* Princeton, NJ: Robert Wood Johnson Foundation.

Singer, T., and V. Engert. 2018. "It Matters What You Practice: Differential Training Effects on Subjective Experience, Behavior, Brain, and Body in the ReSource Project." *Current Opinion in Psychology* 28: 151–58.

Skaalvik, E. M., and S. Skaalvik. 2010. "Teacher Self-Efficacy and Teacher Burnout." *Teaching and Teacher Education* 26: 1059–69.

———. 2015. "Job Satisfaction, Stress, and Coping Strategies in the Teaching Profession: What Do Teachers Say?" *International Education Studies* 8 (3): 181–92.

Small, D. A., G. Loewenstein, and P. Slovic. 2007. "Sympathy and Callousness: The Impact of Deliberative Thought on Donations to Identifiable and Statistical Victims." *Organizational Behavior and Human Decision Processes* 102: 143–53.

Smidt, K. E., and M. K. Suvak. 2015. "A Brief, but Nuanced, Review of Emotional Granularity and Emotion Differentiation Research." *Current Opinion in Psychology* 3: 48–51.

Snyder, C. R. 2002. "Hope Theory: Rainbows in the Mind." *Psychological Inquiry* 13 (4): 249–75.

Souto-Manning, M., and K. Swick. 2006. "Teachers' Beliefs About Parent and Family Involvement." *Early Childhood Education Journal* 34: 187–93.

Spinrad, T. L., and N. Eisenberg. 2009. "Empathy, Prosocial Behavior, and Positive Development in Schools." In *Handbook of Positive Psychology in Schools,* edited by R. Gilman, E. S. Hueber, and M. Furlong. New York: Routledge.

Staats, C. 2016. "Understanding Implicit Bias: What Educators Should Know." *American Educator* 39 (4): 29–33.

Starck, J. G., T. Riddle, S. Sinclair, and N. Warikoo. 2020. "Teachers Are People Too: Examining the Racial Bias of Teachers Compared to Other American Adults." *Educational Researcher* 49 (4): 273–84.

Steele, C. M. 1997. "A Threat in the Air: How Stereotypes Shape Intellectual Identity and Performance." *American Psychologist* 52: 613–29.

———. 2010. *Whistling Vivaldi: How Stereotypes Affect Us and What We Can Do.* New York: Norton.

Steger, M. 2019. "Does a Meaningful Job Need to Burn You Out?" *Greater Good.* https://greatergood .berkeley.edu/article/item/does_a_meaningful_job_need_to_burn_you_out

Stellar, J. E. et al. 2015. "Positive Affect and Markers of Inflammation: Discrete Positive Emotions Predict Lower Levels of Inflammatory Cytokines." *Emotion* 15 (2): 129–33.

Stuckey, H. L., and J. Nobel. 2010. "The Connection Between Art, Healing, and Public Health." *The American Journal of Public Health* 100 (2): 254–63.

Substance Abuse and Mental Health Services Administration: Trauma and Justice Strategic Initiative. 2012. *SAMHSA's Working Definition of Trauma and Guidance for Trauma-Informed Approach.* Rockville, MD: Substance Abuse and Mental Health Services Administration.

Sue, D. W. 2010. *Microaggressions in Everyday Life: Race, Gender, and Sexual Orientation.* Hoboken, NJ: Wiley.

Tajfel, H., and J. C. Turner. 1986. "The Social Identity Theory of Intergroup Behaviour." In *Psychology of Intergroup Relations,* edited by S. Worchel and W. G. Austin. Chicago, IL: Nelson-Hall.

Tal, C. et al. 2019. "The Use of Repeated Narrative Writing by Teachers to Cope with Emotionally Loaded Incidents in the Classroom." In *Teacher Training,* edited by P. E. McDermott. New York: Nova Science.

Tamir, M. et al. 2015. "Desired Emotions Across Cultures: A Value-Based Account." *Journal of Personality and Social Psychology* 111 (1): 67–82.

Tapper, A. J. H. 2013. "A Pedagogy of Social Justice Education: Social Identity Theory, Intersectionality, and Empowerment." *Conflict Resolution Quarterly* 30: 411–45.

Taxer, J. L., and A. C. Frenzel. 2015. "Facets of Teachers' Emotional Lives: A Quantitative Investigation of Teachers' Genuine, Faked, and Hidden Emotions." *Teaching and Teacher Education* 49: 78–88.

Taylor, C. et al. 2016. "Examining Ways That a Mindfulness-Based Intervention Reduces Stress in Public School Teachers." *Mindfulness* 7 (1): 115–29.

Taylor, S. E. 2011. "Social Support: A Review." In *The Oxford Handbook of Health Psychology,* edited by H. S. Friedman. Oxford: Oxford University Press.

Terry, M. L., and M. R. Leary. "Self-Compassion, Self-Regulation, and Health." *Self and Identity* 10 (3): 352–62.

Tinkler, A. S., and B. Tinkler. 2016. "Enhancing Cultural Humility Through Critical Service-Learning in Teacher Preparation." *Multicultural Perspectives* 18 (4): 192–201.

Todd, A. R. et al. 2011. "Perspective Taking Combats Automatic Expressions of Racial Bias." *Journal of Personality and Social Psychology* 100 (6): 1027–42.

Torre, J. B., and M. D. Lieberman. 2018. "Putting Feelings into Words: Affect Labeling as Implicit Emotion Regulation." *Emotion Review* 10 (2): 116–24.

Troy, A. S. et al. 2010. "Seeing the Silver Lining: Cognitive Reappraisal Ability Moderates the Relationship Between Stress and Depressive Symptoms." *Emotion* 10 (6): 783–95.

Tsai, J. L. 2017. "Ideal Affect in Daily Life: Implications for Affective Experience, Health, and Social Behavior." *Current Opinion in Psychology* 17: 118–28.

Tsai J. L., B. Knutson, and H. H. Fung. 2006. "Cultural Variation in Affect Valuation." *Journal of Personality and Social Psychology* 90: 288–307.

Tugade, M. M., and B. L. Fredrickson. 2007. "Regulation of Positive Emotions: Emotion Regulation Strategies That Promote Resilience." *Journal of Happiness Studies* 8: 311–33.

Türktorun, Y. Z., G. M. Weiher, and H. Horz. 2020. "Psychological Detachment and Work-Related Rumination in Teachers." *Educational Research Review* 31: 100354.

Tyrväinen, L. et al. 2013. "The Influence of Urban Green Environments on Stress Relief Measures." *Journal of Environmental Psychology* 38: 1–9.

Van den Bergh, L. et al. 2010. "The Implicit Prejudiced Attitudes of Teachers." *American Educational Research Journal* 47: 497–527.

Van Gordon, W., and E. Shonin. 2020. "Second-Generation Mindfulness-Based Interventions: Toward More Authentic Mindfulness Practice and Teaching." *Mindfulness* 11: 1–4.

Van Tongeren, D. R. et al. 2018. "Heroic Helping: The Effects of Priming Superhero Images on Prosociality." *Frontiers in Psychology* 9: 2243.

Van Wingerden, J., and R. F. Poell. 2019. "Meaningful Work and Resilience Among Teachers." *PLoS ONE* 14 (9): e0222518.

Vehkakoski, T. M. 2020. "'Can do!' Teacher Promotion of Optimism in Response to Student Failure Expectation." *Scandinavian Journal of Educational Research* 64 (3): 408–24.

Walton, G. M., and G. L. Cohen. 2007. "A Question of Belonging: Race, Social Fit, and Achievement." *Journal of Personality and Social Psychology* 92 (1): 82–96.

Walton, G. M., and S. T. Brady. 2021. "The Social-Belonging Intervention." In *Handbook of Wise Interventions: How Social-Psychological Insights Can Help Solve Problems,* edited by G. M. Walton and A. J. Crum. New York: Guilford Press.

Wang, M., and M. Wong. 2014. "Happiness and Leisure Across Countries." *Journal of Happiness Studies* 15: 85–118.

Warren, C. A. 2018. "Empathy, Teacher Dispositions, and Preparation for Culturally Responsive Pedagogy." *Journal of Teacher Education* 69 (2): 169–83.

Waters, L. 2012. "Predicting Job Satisfaction: Contributions of Individual Gratitude and Institutionalized Gratitude." *Psychology* 3: 1174–76.

Waters, L., and H. Stokes. 2015. "Positive Education for School Leaders: Exploring the Effects of Emotion-Gratitude and Action-Gratitude." *The Educational and Developmental Psychologist* 32 (1): 1–22.

Wayment, H. A., A. F. Collier, M. Birkett, T. Traustadóttir, and R. E. Till. 2015. "Brief Quiet Ego Contemplation Reduces Oxidative Stress and Mind-wandering." *Frontiers in Psychology*, 6.

Weger. H., G. C. Bell, E. M. Minei, and M. C. Robinson. 2014. "The Relative Effectiveness of Active Listening in Initial Interactions." *International Journal of Listening* 28 (1): 13–31.

Weinstein, N., and R. M. Ryan. 2010. "When Helping Helps: Autonomous Motivation for Prosocial Behavior and Its Influence on Well-Being for the Helper and Recipient." *Journal of Personality and Social Psychology* 98: 222–44.

Weng, H. Y. et al. 2018. "Visual Attention to Suffering After Compassion Training Is Associated with Decreased Amygdala Responses." *Frontiers in Psychology* 9: 771.

Westermann, K. 2019. "Global Survey Finds We're Lacking Fresh Air and Natural Light as We Spend Less Time in Nature." Velux Media Centre. https://press.velux.com/new-global-survey-finds-were-lacking-fresh-air-and-natural-light-as-we-spend-less-time-in-nature.

Westgate, E. C. 2022. "Art, Music, and Literature: Do the Humanities Make Our Lives Richer, Happier, and More Meaningful?" In *The Oxford Handbook of the Positive Humanities*, edited by L. Tay and J. O. Pawleski. Oxford Handbooks Online. https://www.oxfordhandbooks.com/view/10.1093/oxfordhb/9780190064570.001.0001/oxfordhb-9780190064570-e-1

Wheeler, M. E., and S. T. Fiske. 2005. "Controlling Racial Prejudice: Social-Cognitive Goals Affect Amygdala and Stereotype Activation." *Psychological Science* 16 (1): 56–63.

Whitaker, R. C. et al. 2014. "Adverse Childhood Experiences, Dispositional Mindfulness, and Adult Health." *Preventive Medicine* 67: 147–53.

White, K., M. Stackhouse, and J. J. Argo. 2018. "When Social Identity Threat Leads to the Selection of Identity-Reinforcing Options: The Role of Public Self-Awareness." *Organizational Behavior and Human Decision Processes* 144: 60–73.

White, R. 2012. "A Sociocultural Investigation of the Efficacy of Outdoor Education to Improve Learner Engagement." *Emotional and Behavioural Difficulties* 17 (1): 13–23.

White, R. E., and S. M. Carlson. 2015. "What Would Batman Do? Self-Distancing Improves Executive Function in Young Children." *Developmental Science* 19 (3): 419–26.

Whitford, D. K., and A. M. Emerson. 2019. "Empathy Intervention to Reduce Implicit Bias in Pre-Service Teachers." *Psychological Reports* 122 (2): 670–88.

Willemse, M., and E. Deacon. 2015. "Experiencing a Sense of Calling: The Influence of Meaningful Work on Teachers' Work Attitudes." *SA Journal of Industrial Psychology* 41 (1): 1274.

Willemse, T. M. et al. 2018. Family-School Partnerships: A Challenge for Teacher Education. *Journal of Education for Teaching* 44 (3): 252–57.

Williams, T. O. 2011. "A Poetry Therapy Model for the Literature Classroom." *Journal of Poetry Therapy* 24 (1): 17–33.

Wilson, A., and W. Richardson. 2020. "All I Want to Say Is That They Don't Really Care About Us: Creating and Maintaining Healing-Centered Collective Care in Hostile Times." *Bank Street Occasional Paper Series* (43): 8.

Wood, A. M. et al. 2011. "Using Personal and Psychological Strengths Leads to Increases in Well-Being Over Time." *Personality and Individual Differences* 50: 15–19.

Worthington, E. L. 2020. *The Science of Forgiveness.* John Templeton Foundation. https://www.templeton.org/wp-content/uploads/2020/06/Forgiveness_final.pdf.

Wray-Lake, L., C. DeHaan, J. Shubert, and R. Ryan. 2019. "Examining Links from Civic Engagement to Daily Well-Being from a Self-Determination Theory Perspective." *The Journal of Positive Psychology* 14 (2): 166–77.

Wrzesniewski, A., N. LoBuglio, J. E. Dutton, and J. M. Berg. 2013. "Job Crafting and Cultivating Positive Meaning and Identity in Work." In *Advances in Positive Organizational Psychology,* edited by A. B. Bakker. Bingley, UK: Emerald Group.

Young, S. 2016. "What Is Mindfulness?" In *Handbook of Mindfulness in Education,* edited by K. A. Schonert-Reichl and R. W. Roeser. New York: Springer.

Yu, H. et al. 2020. "Toward a Personality Integration Perspective on Creativity." *The Journal of Positive Psychology* 16, 789–801. https://doi.org/10.1080/17439760.2020.1818810.

Zajoncs, A. 2016. "Contemplation in Education." In *Handbook of Mindfulness in Education,* edited by K. A. Schonert-Reichl and R. W. Roeser. New York: Springer.

Zessin, U., O. Dickhauser, and S. Garbade. 2015. "The Relationship Between Self-Compassion and Well-Being." *Applied Psychology: Health and Well-Being* 7 (3): 340–64.

Zhang, T., Z. Wang, G. Liu, and J. Shao. 2019. "Teachers' Caring Behavior and Problem Behaviors in Adolescents: The Mediating Roles of Cognitive Reappraisal and Expressive Suppression." *Personality and Individual Differences* 142: 270–75.

Zubair, A., and A. Kamal. 2015. "Work Related Flow, Psychological Capital, and Creativity Among Employees of Software Houses." *Psychological Studies* 60: 321–31.

Amy L. Eva, PhD, is associate education director for the Greater Good Science Center at the University of California, Berkeley. As an educational psychologist and teacher educator with decades of experience in classrooms, she writes and speaks about teacher well-being and resilience. She is one of the key developers of Greater Good in Education, which features science-based practices for creating kinder, happier schools. She has also helped to develop free online resources for educators across California while facilitating statewide social-learning communities of practice for educators in collaboration with educational leaders from Sacramento and Orange Counties.

Index

Center for Contemplative Mind in Society, 100, 103

Center for Courage and Renewal, 96, 98

centering exercise, 21

challenges vs. threats, 191

character strengths: affirming your own, 84–86; inventory of values and, 81–82; positive psychology focus on, 80–81, 84, 86; values related to, 81–83

Chen, Siyin, 31

civic behaviors, 177

Clark, Patricia, 115

Coaching for Equity (Aguilar), 78

cognitive behavioral therapy (CBT), 13

cognitive distortions, 13

cognitive reappraisal, 68–69, 70, 127

colleagues: building trust with, 166–168; social support from, 148

Collins, Billy, 99

common humanity, 72

communication, mindful, 138–140

community engagement, 175–177

compassion: power and limits on, 57; practice of, 56–58, 127–129; self-directed, 57, 71–74. See also empathy

complex trauma, 152

concern, empathic, 124–125, 127

connection: mindfulness and human, 31–34; with the natural world, 39–42

contemplation, 43, 44–45; artmaking as, 103; reading as, 100

contribution, meaning of, 88

cortisol, 41, 53, 70, 75

creativity, 95–107; artmaking and, 102–104; benefits of, 98, 101, 104, 107; flow experience and, 105–107; guiding questions about, 97, 100–101, 103, 106–107; poetry reading and, 99–101; third things and, 96–98

Csikszentmihalyi, Mihaly, 105

cultural competence, 119

cultural differences: bridging, 116–118; emotional expression and, 65–66; exercising humility about, 119–121; implicit biases and, 113–115; social identities and, 110–112

cultural-immersion activities, 177

culturally responsive perspective, 172

curiosity, 36–38; creativity and, 105; five dimensions of, 36–37; research on benefits of, 38; resources about, 38; surrendering to, 45

Cutrona, Carolyn, 148

D

Dalai Lama, 58

David, Susan, 59

decisional forgiveness, 53

deficit perspective, 172

demoralization, 1, 56

depersonalization, 51

depression: body scan practice and, 22; cognitive reappraisal and, 68, 70; mindful awareness and, 27

detached awareness, 102

DiAngelo, Robin, 113

Dickinson, Emily, 96, 189

distress, empathic, 124–126, 127

Doyle, Glennon, 50

Duffy, Beth, 112

Dweck, Carol, 186, 187

E

Eckhart, Meister, 104

Egan, Kieran, 48

elaborated anger, 12

Emmons, Robert, 50

emotional contagion, 124

emotional exhaustion, 15, 51, 67

heroes: identifying your personal, 183–184; metaphor of teachers as, 183
hope, 3, 84, 189–191
hostile anger, 13
humility, 119–121, 173, 176

I

Implicit Association Tests, 114–115
implicit biases, 113–115
In the Realm of Hungry Ghosts (Maté), 152
individuation, 88
informational support, 148
inherent dignity, 123
insidious trauma, 158
inspiration, finding, 183–185
instructional mistakes, 186
intergroup contact, 117
interoception, 22
interpersonal mindfulness, 138–140
interpersonal mistakes, 186
intersectionality, 111
intrinsic motivation, 37, 107, 183

J

Jennings, Patricia, 21
job crafting, 92
Jordan, Christian H., 31
journal writing, 9
joy, empathic, 144–146
"joyous exploration" curiosity, 36

K

Kashdan, Todd, 36, 37
Kellogg, Flora, 91
Keltner, Dacher, 46, 47, 57, 141
Killingsworth, Matthew, 19
kindness: practice of, 130–132; self-directed, 72
King, Martin Luther, Jr., 55, 165

Kornfield, Jack, 71
Kuo, Min, 40
Kuttner, Paul, 172

L

labeling emotions, 9
listening, active, 138, 139
loneliness: behavior inspired by, 7; identifying feelings of, 6
Lorde, Audre, 14, 118
Losada, Marcial, 59
loving-kindness practice, 56, 58, 127
Luskin, Fred, 53
Lyubomirsky, Sonja, 15

M

Ma, Yo-Yo, 109
Macy, Joanna, 3
Magee, Rhonda, 151
Malin, Heather, 92
Mapp, Karen, 172
Maté, Gabor, 151, 152
McDonald, Michele, 24
meaningful work: purpose related to, 91, 93; recognizing your own, 87–90
meeting framework, 166–167
memory building, 16
Merton, Thomas, 121
meta-awareness, 27
microaffirmations, 162
microaggressions, 161
mind wandering, 19
mindfulness, 19–34; benefits of, 22, 25–26, 29, 33; body scan practice as, 21–22; guiding questions about, 21, 25, 29, 32–33; human connection related to, 31–34; interpersonal, 138–140; noticing thoughts as, 27–30; observing emotions as, 23–26; resources about, 22, 26, 30, 34;

Real Change *Is* Possible

For more than forty-five years, New Harbinger has published proven-effective self-help books and pioneering workbooks to help readers of all ages and backgrounds improve mental health and well-being, and achieve lasting personal growth. In addition, our spirituality books offer profound guidance for deepening awareness and cultivating healing, self-discovery, and fulfillment.

Founded by psychologist Matthew McKay and Patrick Fanning, New Harbinger is proud to be an independent, employee-owned company. Our books reflect our core values of integrity, innovation, commitment, sustainability, compassion, and trust. Written by leaders in the field and recommended by therapists worldwide, New Harbinger books are practical, accessible, and provide real tools for real change.

 **newharbinger**publications

MORE BOOKS from
NEW HARBINGER PUBLICATIONS

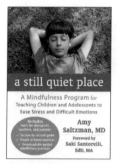

Did you know there are **free tools** you can download for this book?

Free tools are things like **worksheets**, **guided meditation exercises**, and **more** that will help you get the most out of your book.

You can download free tools for this book— whether you bought or borrowed it, in any format, from any source—from the New Harbinger website. All you need is a NewHarbinger.com account. Just use the URL provided in this book to view the free tools that are available for it. Then, click on the "download" button for the free tool you want, and follow the prompts that appear to log in to your NewHarbinger.com account and download the material.

You can also save the free tools for this book to your **Free Tools Library** so you can access them again anytime, just by logging in to your account! Just look for this button on the book's free tools page.

+ Save this to my free tools library